The Ultimate Peach Tree Handbook

How to Grow Peach Trees That Produce the Juiciest Fruits!

An Easy-to-Follow Guide for New Gardeners Looking to Cultivate Healthy and Productive Peach Trees

DID YOU KNOW

> Peaches come in a variety of skin and flesh colors, including yellow, white, and even red. White peaches are sweeter, while yellow ones are tangier.

Table of Contents

Chapter 7: Pruning Your Peach Trees

Chapter 8: Protecting Peach Trees from Pests and Diseases

Chapter 9: Managing Peach Tree Problems

Chapter 10: The Art of Thinning Peaches

Chapter 11: Harvesting Your Peaches

Chapter 12: Health Benefits of Peaches

Chapter 13: Delicious Ways to Enjoy Your Peaches

Chapter 14: Year-Round Peach Tree Care

How to Grow and Care for
Peach Tree

Introduction

Why Grow Peach Trees?

Why Peaches?

Growing peach trees offers an experience that resonates beyond the garden. The peach, often celebrated for its sweet, juicy flavor, has deep roots in many cultures around the world. These fruits have been cherished for centuries, symbolizing everything from longevity to prosperity. Having your own peach tree allows one to not only connect with this rich history but also enjoy the fruits of their labor—literally. There's something almost magical about watching a tree grow from a tiny sapling into a bountiful provider of delicious fruits.

In addition to their delightful taste, peaches are incredibly versatile in the kitchen. They can be eaten fresh off the tree, baked into pies, made into jams, or even grilled for a savory twist. The possibilities are endless, making peaches a favorite among home cooks and professional chefs alike. Growing your own peaches ensures a constant supply of this culinary gem, allowing for creativity in the kitchen that's fueled by the freshest ingredients possible. The ability to experiment with different peach-based recipes adds an exciting dimension to gardening, merging the outdoors with culinary arts.

Peach trees also bring undeniable aesthetic value to any garden. Their blossoms in early spring are a sight to behold, offering a burst of color that signals the end of winter and the beginning of warmer days. These flowers not only attract pollinators like bees and butterflies but also uplift the spirit of anyone who gazes upon them. The beauty of a peach tree in full bloom is a reward in itself, creating a picturesque scene that enhances the overall appeal of your garden space.

Moreover, peach trees are relatively easy to care for, making them an excellent choice for both novice and experienced gardeners. With the right knowledge, which this book will provide, maintaining a healthy and productive peach tree becomes a manageable and enjoyable task. These trees are hardy and adaptable, thriving in a variety of climates, which makes them accessible to a wide range of gardeners. The sense of accomplishment that comes from successfully growing and harvesting peaches is unparalleled.

The health benefits of peaches are another compelling reason to grow these trees. Peaches are rich in vitamins, antioxidants, and fiber, making them a nutritious addition to any diet. Growing your own means having a readily available source of these health benefits right in your backyard. Consuming homegrown peaches not only supports physical well-being but also contributes to a sustainable lifestyle, reducing the need for store-bought fruits that may have been treated with pesticides or traveled long distances.

Peach trees also contribute to environmental well-being by enhancing biodiversity in your garden. They provide habitat and food for various insects and birds, promoting a balanced ecosystem. As a fruit-bearing tree, peaches play a role in the natural cycle of pollination, supporting the health of your garden and surrounding areas. This ecological benefit adds another layer of satisfaction to growing peach trees, as it connects the gardener to the broader environmental impact of their efforts.

The Benefits of Homegrown Peaches

Growing Homegrown Peach Tree

Growing peaches at home offers an array of benefits that extend far beyond the simple pleasure of biting into a fresh, juicy fruit. One of the most significant advantages is the ability to control the growing conditions of your peach trees. This control means that you can ensure your peaches are free from harmful pesticides and chemicals, making them safer and healthier to eat. With homegrown peaches, you know exactly what goes into the growing process, from the type of fertilizer used to the watering schedule, providing peace of mind that your fruits are as natural and organic as possible.

Homegrown peaches also tend to be fresher and more flavorful than store-bought varieties. Commercially grown peaches are often picked before they are fully ripe to withstand shipping and extend shelf life. However, this early picking can compromise flavor and texture. When you grow your own peaches, you can wait until they are perfectly ripe before harvesting, ensuring that they are at their peak sweetness and juiciness. This freshness translates to a superior taste that is hard to match with store-bought fruit.

Another benefit of growing peaches at home is the cost savings. While there is an initial investment in purchasing a peach tree and setting up your garden, the long-term savings can be substantial. Once your peach tree starts producing fruit, you'll have a steady supply of fresh peaches each season without the need to buy them from the store. Considering the cost of organic peaches, growing your own can be a financially savvy decision that pays off year after year.

Homegrown peaches also offer the convenience of having fresh fruit readily available whenever you want it. No more trips to the store or waiting for the right season to enjoy your favorite fruit. With a peach tree in your backyard, you can simply step outside and pick a fresh peach whenever the craving strikes. This convenience also extends to preserving peaches for later use, whether through canning, freezing, or drying, ensuring you have a supply of peaches long after the growing season has ended.

The environmental benefits of growing peaches at home should not be overlooked. By growing your own fruit, you reduce your carbon footprint by eliminating the need for transportation and packaging associated with store-bought peaches. Additionally, a peach tree can contribute to your garden's overall health by improving soil quality, supporting pollinators, and providing shade for other plants. This holistic approach to gardening creates a more sustainable and eco-friendly environment, which is a benefit for both the gardener and the planet.

Cultivating peach trees at home also fosters a deeper connection to the food you eat. There is something profoundly satisfying about nurturing a tree from a small sapling to a mature, fruit-bearing plant. This process encourages a greater appreciation for the natural world and the effort required to produce food. It's a rewarding experience that can also be shared with family and friends, creating memories that last a lifetime. Sharing homegrown peaches with loved ones adds a personal touch to any meal, making the fruits of your labor even sweeter.

Finally, growing your own peaches can lead to a healthier lifestyle overall. The physical activity involved in planting, pruning, and harvesting peach trees provides a form of exercise that can improve fitness and well-being. Additionally, having a supply of fresh, healthy fruit on hand encourages healthier eating habits. Peaches are naturally low in calories and high in nutrients, making them a perfect snack or ingredient in a balanced diet. The act of growing and consuming your own fruit can inspire a more mindful approach to health and nutrition, benefiting both body and mind.

What This Book Will Teach You

This book is designed to be your go-to resource for all things related to growing peach trees, whether you're a complete beginner or have some gardening experience under your belt. The journey begins with an in-depth understanding of peach trees, including their history, varieties, and the basic biology that makes these trees so special. This foundational knowledge will equip you with the confidence to start your peach-growing adventure on the right foot.

One of the key aspects of this book is its focus on the practicalities of growing peach trees. You'll find detailed guidance on selecting the right variety for your garden, preparing your soil, and planting your tree. Each step is broken down into easy-to-follow instructions, ensuring that you can successfully navigate the challenges of getting your peach tree established. Whether you're working with a large garden or a small urban space, this book has tips and tricks tailored to your specific situation.

As you progress, the book delves into the art of caring for your peach tree throughout its life cycle. This includes essential practices such as watering, feeding, and pruning, which are crucial for maintaining a healthy and productive tree. The book also covers more advanced topics like pest control and disease prevention, providing you with the knowledge needed to tackle any issues that may arise. With this information, you'll be well-prepared to keep your peach tree thriving year after year.

One of the unique features of this book is its emphasis on the health benefits of peaches and how to maximize these through home growing. You'll learn about the nutritional content of peaches and how they can contribute to a healthy diet. The book also explores various ways to enjoy your homegrown peaches, from fresh eating to preserving and cooking. This holistic approach ensures that you not only grow delicious peaches but also fully appreciate their role in a healthy lifestyle.

Throughout the book, you'll find a wealth of tips and insights gained from years of experience in peach tree cultivation. These nuggets of wisdom are designed to help you avoid common pitfalls and make the most of your peach-growing journey. The book also encourages a sustainable approach to gardening, offering advice on organic methods and eco-friendly practices. By the end of your reading, you'll not only be equipped to grow peach trees successfully but also to do so in a way that benefits both you and the environment.

Another highlight of this book is its user-friendly structure. Each chapter is organized to build on the previous one, creating a logical flow that guides you through the entire process of growing peach trees. The subchapters provide in-depth information on specific topics, allowing you to easily find the details you need when you need them. This layout makes the book a practical reference that you can return to time and time again as your peach trees grow and develop.

This book is more than just a gardening guide—it's a companion on your peach-growing journey. It aims to inspire, educate, and support you as you embark on this rewarding endeavor. Whether you're planting your first peach tree or looking to improve your existing orchard, this book offers the knowledge and encouragement needed to succeed. Get ready to transform your garden into a haven of delicious, homegrown peaches, and enjoy the many rewards that come with it.

Chapter 1

Understanding Peach Trees

The Origins of Peach Trees

Peach trees have a fascinating history that dates back thousands of years. The origins of the peach, scientifically known as *Prunus persica*, can be traced to China, where it has been cultivated since ancient times. The fruit was highly prized in Chinese culture, symbolizing immortality and unity, and was often featured in art, literature, and mythology. From China, the peach spread along the Silk Road to Persia, where it was given the name "persica," and from there, it made its way to Europe and eventually to the Americas.

The journey of the peach tree across continents is a testament to its adaptability and appeal. In Persia, now modern-day Iran, the peach thrived in the region's climate and became an integral part of local agriculture. The Persians further refined the cultivation techniques, which were later adopted by the Greeks and Romans. The Romans, in particular, played a crucial role in spreading peach cultivation throughout Europe. They valued the fruit not only for its taste but also for its perceived medicinal properties.

During the Age of Exploration, European settlers introduced the peach to the Americas. Spanish explorers brought peach seeds to Florida in the 16th century, where the tree quickly took root. As settlers moved westward, so did the peach, finding new homes in various regions of North America. The fruit became a staple in many American gardens and orchards, admired for its sweet flavor and versatility. Today, the United States is one of the largest producers of peaches, with states like Georgia, South Carolina, and California leading the way.

Growing Peach Trees in a Home Garden

The global spread of peach trees has resulted in a wide variety of cultivars, each adapted to specific climates and growing conditions. This diversity has allowed peaches to thrive in many different environments, from temperate regions to warmer, subtropical areas. The long history of peach cultivation has also led to the development of numerous cultural practices and traditions surrounding the fruit, making it a symbol of abundance and hospitality in many cultures.

The story of the peach tree is also one of innovation and improvement. Over the centuries, farmers and horticulturists have worked to breed new varieties of peaches with better flavors, textures, and resistance to diseases. These efforts have led to the peaches we enjoy today, which are not only delicious but also more resilient and easier to grow. Understanding the origins of the peach tree helps to appreciate the rich heritage and ongoing efforts to cultivate this beloved fruit.

Peach trees have become so integrated into the agricultural landscapes of many countries that it's easy to forget their exotic beginnings. However, the history of the peach is a reminder of the interconnectedness of global agriculture and the shared knowledge that has shaped the way we grow and enjoy this fruit. The origins of peach trees are a vital part of their story, adding depth to the experience of cultivating and consuming peaches in the modern world.

Types of Peach Trees

Peach trees come in a wide variety of types, each offering unique characteristics that cater to different growing conditions and consumer preferences. The most common distinction among peach types is between freestone and clingstone varieties. Freestone peaches are those where the flesh easily separates from the pit, making them ideal for eating fresh and for culinary uses such as baking and canning. Clingstone peaches, on the other hand, have flesh that clings tightly to the pit, which makes them excellent for processing into products like jams and preserves.

In addition to freestone and clingstone, peaches are also categorized based on their flesh color, which can range from yellow to white. Yellow-fleshed peaches are more common in the United States and have a tangy-sweet flavor with a slight acidity. These peaches are often favored for their bold taste and are widely used in cooking and baking. White-fleshed peaches, which are more popular in Asian countries, have a sweeter, less acidic flavor and are often eaten fresh. The delicate taste of white peaches makes them a favorite for those who prefer a milder, more aromatic fruit.

Another important type of peach is the donut or flat peach, known for its unique shape and sweet, succulent flavor. Donut peaches are a relatively recent addition to the market, having gained popularity in the last few decades. Their flattened, saucer-like shape sets them apart from traditional round peaches, and their sweet, low-acid flesh makes them a delightful snack. These peaches are often enjoyed fresh, but they can also be used in desserts and salads for a unique twist.

In colder climates, gardeners often opt for cold-hardy peach varieties that can withstand lower temperatures. These types of peaches have been bred to survive in regions with harsh winters, where traditional peach trees might not thrive. Some examples of cold-hardy peach varieties include the Reliance and Contender peaches, which are known for their ability to produce fruit even after a late spring frost. Growing these varieties expands the geographic range of peach cultivation, allowing more people to enjoy homegrown peaches.

Dwarf peach trees are another type that is becoming increasingly popular, especially for those with limited space. These trees are bred to remain small, making them perfect for container gardening or small urban gardens.

Despite their size, dwarf peach trees can produce full-sized fruit with the same quality as their larger counterparts. This makes them an excellent choice for gardeners who want to enjoy fresh peaches without the need for a large garden or orchard.

Peach trees are also classified based on their blooming period, which can be early, mid, or late-season. Early-blooming varieties produce fruit sooner in the growing season, making them ideal for regions with short summers. Mid and late-season peaches, on the other hand, extend the harvest period, allowing for a continuous supply of fresh peaches throughout the summer. Choosing the right type of peach tree based on bloom time can help ensure a longer and more abundant harvest.

Understanding the different types of peach trees is crucial for selecting the right variety for your garden. Each type offers its own set of advantages, whether it's the ease of processing with freestone peaches, the unique flavor of white-fleshed varieties, or the practicality of cold-hardy or dwarf trees. By familiarizing yourself with these types, you can make an informed decision that aligns with your climate, space, and taste preferences, setting the stage for a successful peach-growing experience.

Peach Tree Anatomy

The anatomy of a peach tree is a fascinating study of how each part contributes to the growth and fruit production of this beloved tree. Starting with the roots, peach trees have a relatively shallow root system that spreads out widely rather than deeply. This root structure allows the tree to efficiently absorb water and nutrients from the soil. However, it also makes the tree more susceptible to drought and soil compaction, which is why proper soil preparation and watering practices are essential for healthy growth.

Moving up from the roots, the trunk of the peach tree serves as the main support structure, connecting the roots to the branches and leaves. The trunk also acts as a conduit for transporting water, nutrients, and sugars between the roots and the rest of the tree. As the tree matures, the trunk thickens and develops bark, which protects the tree from physical damage and disease. Pruning the trunk and main branches is crucial for maintaining the tree's shape and ensuring adequate sunlight penetration to all parts of the tree.

The branches of a peach tree play a vital role in supporting the leaves and fruit. These branches must be strong enough to bear the weight of the peaches as they develop, which is why proper pruning is so important. The angle at which branches grow from the trunk can affect their strength and the overall structure of the tree. Branches that grow at a wider angle from the trunk are generally stronger and better able to support heavy fruit loads. Regular pruning helps to promote these strong, well-angled branches, which are key to a productive peach tree.

Leaves are the powerhouses of the peach tree, responsible for photosynthesis—the process of converting sunlight into energy for the tree's growth and fruit production. Peach tree leaves are typically lance-shaped and have serrated edges. They are usually bright green, which is a sign of a healthy, functioning photosynthesis process. The leaves also play a role in transpiration, where water is released into the atmosphere, helping to cool the tree and maintain nutrient uptake from the roots.

Flowering is one of the most visually striking aspects of peach tree anatomy. The flowers, which bloom in early spring, are usually pink or light red and are crucial for the tree's reproductive process. Each flower has both male (stamens) and female (pistil) reproductive organs, allowing for self-pollination in many peach varieties. However, pollinators such as bees also play an essential role in ensuring successful fruit set. The timing of the bloom is critical, as late frosts can damage the flowers and reduce the fruit yield.

The fruit itself is the most anticipated part of the peach tree. A peach is a type of stone fruit, meaning it has a hard pit or stone in the center, surrounded by juicy flesh and a thin, fuzzy skin. The development of the fruit begins with pollination, followed by the formation of the ovary, which eventually matures into the peach. As the fruit grows, it undergoes several stages of development, from the green, immature stage to the fully ripe, sweet, and juicy stage that we enjoy eating.

Each part of the peach tree—from the roots to the leaves, flowers, and fruit—works in harmony to ensure the tree's survival and productivity. Understanding the anatomy of a peach tree is essential for effective cultivation, as it allows for better management of growth, disease prevention, and fruit production.

Chapter 2

Choosing the Perfect Peach Tree for Your Garden

Climate Considerations

When selecting a peach tree for your garden, understanding the climate is crucial. Peach trees require specific conditions to thrive, and choosing a variety that matches your local climate can make the difference between a bountiful harvest and a disappointing season. One of the primary factors to consider is the chill hours, which refers to the number of hours below 45°F that a peach tree needs during the dormant winter period. This chilling requirement varies among different peach varieties and is essential for proper bud development and fruit set.

In regions with mild winters, selecting a peach tree with a low chill hour requirement is important. Varieties that need fewer chill hours will bloom and produce fruit even with limited winter cold. On the other hand, in areas with colder winters, peach trees with higher chill hour requirements are more suitable. These trees are adapted to withstand prolonged cold periods and will not break dormancy too early, which could expose them to late frosts that can damage the flowers and reduce fruit yield.

Temperature extremes are another crucial aspect of climate that affects peach tree selection. Peach trees are sensitive to both excessive heat and cold. In hot climates, choosing a heat-tolerant variety is key to preventing heat stress, which can lead to fruit drop and poor-quality peaches. In contrast, in regions with harsh winters, selecting a cold-hardy variety ensures that the tree can survive freezing temperatures without suffering significant damage. Some peach trees are bred specifically for extreme climates, offering resilience against temperature fluctuations.

Humidity levels also play a role in peach tree health. High humidity can increase the risk of fungal diseases such as peach leaf curl and brown rot. In humid climates, it's beneficial to select disease-resistant peach varieties that are less susceptible to these issues. Additionally, proper tree spacing and pruning to improve air circulation can help mitigate the effects of high humidity on peach tree health. Understanding your local humidity conditions and choosing the right variety can help prevent disease-related problems.

Another factor to consider is the length of the growing season. Peach trees require a long, warm growing season to produce mature fruit. In regions with shorter growing seasons, early-maturing peach varieties are preferable. These varieties ripen quickly, allowing for a successful harvest before the onset of cooler temperatures in the fall. Conversely, in areas with extended growing seasons, mid to late-season varieties can be grown to take advantage of the full growing period, providing a prolonged harvest.

The microclimate of your garden should also be taken into account when selecting a peach tree. Factors such as soil temperature, wind exposure, and sunlight availability can vary significantly within a small area. For example, a south-facing slope might offer more warmth and sunlight, making it an ideal location for a peach tree. Conversely, a low-lying area may be prone to frost pockets, which could damage the tree during spring frosts. Understanding the specific conditions of your garden will help you choose a variety that is well-suited to thrive in that environment.

Considering these climate factors when selecting a peach tree ensures that the tree is well-adapted to its growing environment. Matching the tree's needs with your local climate not only increases the chances of a successful harvest but also reduces the need for extensive interventions, such as frost protection or disease management. With the right climate considerations in mind, selecting the perfect peach tree for your garden becomes a more informed and confident process.

Soil Requirements

The success of growing peach trees heavily relies on the quality of the soil in which they are planted. Peach trees thrive in well-drained, sandy loam soils with a pH range of 6.0 to 7.5. Soil that drains well is crucial because peach trees are particularly sensitive to waterlogged conditions. Excess moisture in the soil can lead to root rot and other fungal diseases, which can severely impact the health of the tree and its ability to produce fruit. Ensuring proper drainage is the first step in preparing your soil for peach tree cultivation.

To assess whether your soil has good drainage, a simple test can be conducted. Dig a hole about a foot deep and fill it with water. If the water drains within a few hours, the soil has adequate drainage. However, if the water remains in the hole for an extended period, it indicates poor drainage, and steps will need to be taken to improve it. Adding organic matter such as compost or well-rotted manure can enhance soil structure, improve drainage, and increase nutrient availability, creating an ideal environment for peach tree roots to thrive.

Soil pH is another critical factor in peach tree health. The pH level affects the availability of essential nutrients in the soil. Peach trees prefer a slightly acidic to neutral pH, which allows them to absorb nutrients efficiently. If the soil pH is too high (alkaline) or too low (acidic), the tree may suffer from nutrient deficiencies, even if the soil is rich in those nutrients. Conducting a soil test is recommended to determine the pH level of your soil. If adjustments are needed, lime can be added to raise the pH, or sulfur can be applied to lower it.

In addition to pH, the nutrient content of the soil is crucial for peach tree growth. Peach trees require a balanced supply of macronutrients, including nitrogen (N), phosphorus (P), and potassium (K), as well as essential micronutrients like iron, zinc, and manganese. Soil tests can also reveal nutrient deficiencies, allowing for targeted fertilization to correct any imbalances. Organic fertilizers, such as compost and manure, are excellent choices for providing a slow-release source of nutrients that improve soil fertility over time.

While sandy loam is ideal, not all gardens have naturally occurring soil of this type. However, soil texture can be modified to better suit peach trees. For heavy clay soils, incorporating organic matter and sand can improve aeration and drainage. In sandy soils that drain too quickly, adding compost can help retain moisture and nutrients. Mulching around the base of the tree also aids in moisture retention and temperature regulation, providing a more stable environment for the roots.

Another consideration is the depth of the soil. Peach trees require a deep soil profile to accommodate their root system, which can extend several feet below the surface. Shallow or compacted soils can restrict root growth, leading to poor tree development and reduced fruit production. If your garden has shallow soil, consider planting on a raised bed to provide the necessary depth for the roots to expand. This approach can also improve drainage and prevent waterlogging.

Preparing the soil properly before planting a peach tree sets the foundation for its long-term health and productivity. By addressing factors such as drainage, pH, nutrient content, and soil depth, you create an environment that supports vigorous growth and abundant fruiting. Investing time in soil preparation ensures that your peach tree has the best possible start, leading to a healthier tree and a more fruitful harvest.

Selecting the Right Variety

Choosing the right variety of peach tree is a critical decision that can greatly influence the success of your peach-growing endeavors. With hundreds of peach varieties available, each with its own unique characteristics, making the right choice requires careful consideration of factors such as climate, growing conditions, and personal preferences. Understanding the distinctions between different varieties helps to ensure that the tree you select will thrive in your garden and meet your expectations for fruit quality and yield.

One of the first factors to consider when selecting a peach variety is the tree's chill hour requirement. Chill hours refer to the number of hours below 45°F that a peach tree needs to break dormancy and set fruit. This requirement varies widely among varieties, from as few as 150 chill hours to more than 1,000. It is essential to match the chill hour requirement of the variety to your local climate. If the tree does not receive enough chill hours, it may not produce fruit, while too many chill hours can cause early blooming, which increases the risk of frost damage.

The flavor and texture of the fruit are also important considerations when selecting a peach variety. Some peaches are prized for their sweet, juicy flesh and are best enjoyed fresh, while others are better suited for baking, canning, or making preserves. Freestone varieties, where the flesh easily separates from the pit, are often preferred for fresh eating and culinary uses. Clingstone varieties, with flesh that clings to the pit, are typically used for processing and are favored for their firmness and sweetness in canned goods. White-fleshed peaches offer a milder, sweeter taste compared to the more acidic yellow-fleshed varieties, making them a popular choice for those who prefer a subtler flavor.

Disease resistance is another crucial factor in selecting a peach variety. Some varieties are more resistant to common peach diseases such as peach leaf curl, brown rot, and bacterial spot. Choosing a disease-resistant variety can reduce the need for chemical treatments and make tree care easier,

21

particularly for organic gardeners. Researching the disease resistance of different varieties and selecting one that is well-suited to your region can help prevent potential problems and promote a healthier tree.

Harvest time is an additional consideration when choosing a peach variety. Peaches ripen at different times throughout the growing season, with early-season varieties maturing as soon as May or June, while late-season varieties may not be ready until August or September. Depending on your climate and preferences, selecting an early, mid, or late-season variety—or a combination of all three—can help you extend the harvest period and enjoy fresh peaches throughout the summer. This staggered approach to planting can provide a continuous supply of ripe fruit over several months.

The size of the tree is another factor to consider, especially if space is limited. Standard peach trees can grow quite large, often reaching heights of 20 feet or more. However, there are also dwarf and semi-dwarf varieties that remain smaller, typically growing to around 8 to 12 feet tall. These smaller trees are ideal for home gardens with limited space and are easier to manage and harvest. Despite their size, dwarf and semi-dwarf trees can produce full-sized fruit with the same quality and flavor as larger trees.

When selecting a peach variety, it's also worth considering the tree's growth habit and aesthetic appeal. Some varieties are known for their showy blossoms, which add ornamental value to the garden in early spring. Others may have unique features such as red or bronze foliage, providing additional visual interest. The overall shape of the tree, whether spreading, upright, or compact, can also influence how it fits into your garden design.

Chapter 3

Preparing Your Garden for Peach Trees

Site Selection

Peach trees grow best in areas with plenty of direct sunlight.

Choosing the right site for planting peach trees is one of the most critical decisions in ensuring a healthy and productive orchard. Peach trees thrive in locations that receive full sunlight, which means at least six to eight hours of direct sunlight daily. The sun's energy is vital for photosynthesis, the process through which trees produce the energy needed for growth and fruit development. A sunny location not only enhances fruit quality but also reduces the likelihood of disease, as sunlight helps keep the foliage dry, minimizing the risk of fungal infections.

In addition to sunlight, peach trees require good air circulation. Proper airflow around the tree helps to prevent moisture from lingering on the leaves and fruit, which can reduce the occurrence of diseases like peach leaf curl and brown rot. When selecting a site, avoid areas that are too enclosed by buildings or other trees, as these can block air movement. Open areas on a gentle slope are ideal, as they allow cold air to drain away from the trees, reducing the risk of frost damage in the spring.

Another crucial factor in site selection is the soil type and drainage. Peach trees prefer well-drained, sandy loam soils that prevent water from pooling around the roots. Standing water can lead to root rot and other issues that can severely impact tree health. If the soil in your chosen site tends to be heavy clay or poorly drained, consider amending it with organic matter or creating raised beds to improve drainage. Ensuring that water drains away from the roots is key to maintaining a healthy tree.

The site's proximity to water sources is also important. Peach trees require regular watering, especially during the growing season, so having a nearby water source makes irrigation more convenient. However, the site should not be prone to waterlogging or located in low-lying areas where water may accumulate. The balance between accessibility to water and proper drainage is essential for successful peach tree cultivation.

Consider the space available at the site when planning for your peach trees. Peach trees need room to grow both above and below ground. Standard-sized peach trees can spread up to 20 feet in diameter, while dwarf varieties may require about 10 to 12 feet of space. Ensure that the site provides enough room for the tree's canopy to expand without competition from other plants or structures. Adequate spacing is crucial for sunlight penetration, air circulation, and root development.

The microclimate of the site should also be evaluated. Microclimates are small areas within a larger environment that have slightly different conditions, such as temperature or humidity levels. South-facing slopes are often warmer and more protected from cold winds, making them ideal for peach trees. Avoid planting in frost pockets or areas prone to late spring frosts, as these can damage the blossoms and reduce fruit yield. Understanding the microclimate of your garden can help you select the best location for your peach trees.

Soil Preparation and Testing

Proper soil preparation is essential for the successful establishment and growth of peach trees. The first step in preparing the soil is to assess its current condition, including texture, pH, and nutrient content. Soil testing is an invaluable tool that provides detailed information about these characteristics. A standard soil test will reveal the pH level, which is crucial for nutrient availability, as well as the levels of key nutrients such as nitrogen, phosphorus, and potassium. Testing also helps identify any deficiencies or toxicities that need to be addressed before planting.

Once the soil test results are in, the next step is to adjust the soil pH if necessary. Peach trees prefer a slightly acidic to neutral pH range of 6.0 to 7.5. If the soil is too acidic (low pH), lime can be added to raise the pH. Conversely, if the soil is too alkaline (high pH), elemental sulfur or organic matter can be used to lower it. Adjusting the pH to the optimal range ensures that the peach tree roots can effectively absorb the nutrients they need for healthy growth and fruit production.

Improving soil structure is another critical aspect of soil preparation. Peach trees thrive in well-drained, sandy loam soils, but not all gardens naturally have this ideal soil type. For soils that are too heavy or clayey, adding organic matter such as compost, well-rotted manure, or leaf mold can improve texture and drainage. Organic matter also enhances soil fertility by providing a slow-release source of nutrients and increasing microbial activity. Incorporating sand or perlite can further improve drainage in heavy soils, creating a more favorable environment for peach tree roots.

For sandy soils that drain too quickly, the challenge is to retain moisture and nutrients. In these cases, adding organic matter is again beneficial, as it helps the soil hold water and nutrients longer, reducing the frequency of irrigation and fertilization. Mulching around the base of the tree with organic materials like straw, wood chips, or composted leaves can also help conserve moisture and regulate soil temperature, promoting healthier root growth.

In addition to soil texture and pH, the nutrient content of the soil must be addressed. Based on the soil test results, amendments can be added to correct any nutrient deficiencies. Nitrogen is crucial for vegetative growth, phosphorus supports root development and fruit production, and potassium is important for overall tree health and resistance to disease. Balanced fertilizers or specific nutrient amendments can be incorporated into the soil before planting to ensure that the peach tree has access to the nutrients it needs.

Soil preparation should also consider the physical condition of the soil. Compacted soil can restrict root growth and reduce the tree's ability to access water and nutrients. If the soil is compacted, it may be necessary to till or aerate the soil to loosen it before planting. However, care should be taken not to over-till, as this can disrupt soil structure and lead to erosion. The goal is to create a loose, friable soil that allows roots to penetrate deeply and establish a strong foundation.

Planning for Growth

When planning for the growth of peach trees, it's essential to consider the long-term needs of the trees as they mature. Peach trees can live for several decades, so their placement in the garden should account for both current and future growth. One of the first considerations is the spacing between trees. Proper spacing is critical to ensure that each tree has enough room to expand its canopy, access sunlight, and develop a strong root system. Standard peach trees typically require about 20 feet of spacing between each other, while dwarf varieties may need around 10 to 12 feet.

The direction of planting also plays a role in the tree's growth. In regions with hot climates, it's beneficial to orient the rows of peach trees in a north-south direction. This orientation maximizes sunlight exposure throughout the day, allowing the trees to receive even light on all sides. In cooler climates, an east-west orientation might be preferred to capture the early morning sun, which can help dry dew on the leaves and reduce the risk of fungal diseases. Understanding the sun's path and how it affects your garden can inform the best planting direction for optimal growth.

Consideration should also be given to the future height and spread of the peach trees. As the trees grow, they will require more space above and below ground. The root system of a mature peach tree can extend well beyond the canopy's drip line, so it's important to ensure that there are no obstacles such as buildings, pathways, or underground utilities that could interfere with root expansion. Planning for these spatial requirements from the beginning helps avoid potential problems as the tree matures.

In addition to physical space, the growing peach trees will need sufficient access to water and nutrients. Installing a drip irrigation system during the initial planting phase can help ensure that each tree receives consistent moisture, which is crucial for growth, especially during dry periods. Drip irrigation is efficient and reduces water waste by delivering water directly to the root zone. Planning for irrigation needs early on can save time and effort in the long run, and it contributes to healthier, more productive trees.

Pruning and training the trees are also important aspects of planning for growth. Peach trees benefit from regular pruning to maintain their shape, encourage airflow, and promote fruit production. When planting, it's helpful to consider how the trees will be pruned in the future and to plan for easy access to all parts of the tree. This might involve creating pathways or spacing the trees in a way that allows for easy movement around them. Planning for these maintenance tasks ensures that the trees can be properly cared for as they grow.

Planning should also take into account the potential for disease and pest management. Peach trees are susceptible to various pests and diseases, so it's wise to anticipate these challenges and plan accordingly. This might include selecting disease-resistant varieties, implementing preventive measures such as proper spacing and sanitation, and preparing for the possibility of applying organic or chemical treatments. Being proactive in planning for these aspects of growth can reduce the likelihood of severe infestations or infections that could impact tree health.

Incorporating companion planting into the planning process can further enhance the growth and health of peach trees. Certain plants, such as marigolds, garlic, and nasturtiums, can help deter pests or improve soil health when planted near peach trees. Planning for these companion plants alongside your peach trees can create a more resilient and balanced garden ecosystem. As you plan for the growth of your peach trees, considering these various factors will contribute to a thriving orchard that rewards you with abundant, delicious fruit.

Chapter 4

Planting Your Peach Tree

When and How to Plant

Carefully planting a peach tree is crucial for its growth and fruiting success

Timing and technique are crucial when it comes to planting peach trees. The best time to plant peach trees is during their dormant season, which typically falls in late winter to early spring. Planting during dormancy allows the tree to establish its root system before the demands of spring growth begin. In regions with mild winters, planting can also be done in the fall, giving the tree time to acclimate before the colder months. Choosing the right time for planting helps minimize transplant shock and sets the stage for vigorous growth.

Before planting, it's important to prepare the planting site properly. Start by digging a hole that is wide and deep enough to accommodate the root system of the tree. The hole should be at least twice as wide as the root ball and deep enough so that the tree sits at the same depth it was growing in the nursery. For bare-root trees, the hole should be deep enough to allow the roots to spread out naturally. Properly sized planting holes give the roots space to grow and access to nutrients and water.

When placing the tree in the hole, it's essential to position it correctly. The tree should be placed so that the graft union (the bulge where the tree was grafted onto the rootstock) is about 2 to 3 inches above the soil line. This prevents the scion (the upper part of the grafted tree) from taking root, which could negate the benefits of the rootstock, such as disease resistance or size control. Ensuring the correct planting depth helps the tree establish itself properly and promotes healthy growth.

Backfilling the hole with soil is the next step, and it should be done with care. Gently pack the soil around the roots, ensuring that there are no air pockets, which can dry out the roots. Avoid adding fertilizers or amendments directly into the planting hole, as these can burn the roots and hinder establishment. Instead, use the native soil to backfill, and save any soil amendments for top dressing or incorporating into the wider planting area after the tree has settled.

Watering the newly planted tree is critical to help it establish roots. After backfilling, water the tree thoroughly to settle the soil around the roots and eliminate any remaining air pockets. A slow, deep watering encourages the roots to grow downward and helps the tree adapt to its new environment. It's important to keep the soil consistently moist but not waterlogged during the first few weeks after planting, as this is when the tree is most vulnerable to transplant shock.

Mulching around the base of the tree is a beneficial practice that helps retain soil moisture, suppress weeds, and regulate soil temperature. Apply a layer of mulch about 2 to 3 inches thick around the tree, extending out to the drip line. However, be sure to keep the mulch a few inches away from the trunk to prevent rot and pest issues. Mulching provides a buffer against environmental stresses and creates a more favorable environment for root growth.

Bare-Root vs. Container Trees

When it comes to planting peach trees, gardeners have the option of choosing between bare-root and container-grown trees. Each type has its advantages and considerations, and understanding these can help in making the best choice for your garden. Bare-root trees are typically more affordable and are available during the dormant season. These trees are sold without soil around their roots, which makes them easier to transport and handle. Bare-root trees often establish more quickly because they don't have the constraints of a container, allowing their roots to spread out naturally in the soil.

One of the primary advantages of bare-root trees is their lighter weight and easier handling. Without the added weight of soil, these trees are easier to transport and plant, which can be particularly beneficial if multiple trees are being planted. Additionally, bare-root trees tend to have a broader selection available from nurseries, especially heirloom or specialized varieties that might not be as commonly available in containers. This wider selection allows gardeners to choose the exact variety that best suits their climate and preferences.

Planting bare-root trees requires careful attention to timing and soil conditions. Because they are sold during dormancy, bare-root trees must be planted before they break dormancy and begin to leaf out. This means that the window for planting is relatively narrow, typically from late winter to early spring. Properly storing the trees before planting is also essential to prevent the roots from drying out. Bare-root trees should be soaked in water for a few hours before planting to rehydrate the roots and ensure successful establishment.

Container-grown trees, on the other hand, are available throughout the year and are sold with their roots already established in soil. This makes them more flexible in terms of planting time, as they can be planted at almost any time of year, provided that the ground is not frozen. Container trees are often easier to plant because their roots are already acclimated to growing in soil. This reduces the risk of transplant shock, which can be a concern with bare-root trees, especially if they are not handled or planted correctly.

One of the advantages of container-grown trees is that they are often larger and more established at the time of purchase. This can lead to faster fruit production, as the tree may be closer to maturity than a bare-root counterpart. Container trees are also less vulnerable to environmental stresses during transport and planting since their roots are protected by the soil in the container. This protection can make them a more forgiving option for novice gardeners or those planting in challenging conditions.

However, container trees can come with certain drawbacks. The roots may become pot-bound or develop circling roots if they have been in the container for too long. These root issues can hinder the tree's ability to establish itself once planted in the garden. It's important to inspect the roots before planting and to gently tease them apart if they are tightly wound. This encourages the roots to grow outward into the surrounding soil, which is crucial for the tree's long-term health.

Choosing between bare-root and container-grown peach trees depends on various factors, including planting time, tree size, and personal preference. Bare-root trees offer a cost-effective and lightweight option, with the potential for quicker establishment if planted correctly. Container-grown trees provide flexibility in planting time and may lead to faster fruit production, but they require careful attention to root health during planting. Understanding these options allows gardeners to make an informed decision that aligns with their goals and gardening conditions.

Staking and Mulching

Staking is an important step in supporting young peach trees, especially in areas with strong winds or in the case of trees with weaker root systems. Staking helps to stabilize the tree while it establishes its roots in the new environment, reducing the risk of the tree being blown over or leaning as it grows. When staking a peach tree, it's important to do so correctly to avoid damaging the trunk or hindering the tree's natural movement, which is essential for developing a strong trunk and root system.

Staking and Mulching Peach Tree For Stability and Health

To stake a peach tree, use a sturdy stake made of wood or metal, and drive it into the ground about 6 inches away from the trunk. The stake should be positioned on the windward side of the tree to provide the most support against prevailing winds. The height of the stake should be about two-thirds of the tree's height, providing adequate support without restricting the tree's natural sway. This sway is important as it encourages the tree to develop a strong, resilient trunk.

When tying the tree to the stake, use a flexible, soft material that won't cut into the bark or restrict the tree's growth. Materials like tree ties, soft cloth, or rubber tubing are ideal for this purpose. Tie the tree loosely to the stake, allowing it to move slightly in the wind while still being supported. Avoid using wire or other hard materials that could damage the tree's bark. The goal is to provide support without causing injury or impeding the tree's natural development.

Staking is generally a temporary measure and should be removed after one or two growing seasons. As the tree's roots establish and the trunk strengthens, the tree will no longer need the additional support. Leaving the stake in place for too long can lead to dependency, where the tree fails to develop a strong enough trunk and root system to support itself. Removing the stake at the appropriate time ensures that the tree can grow independently and remain healthy in the long term.

Mulching around the base of the peach tree offers several benefits that contribute to the tree's health and growth. A layer of mulch helps to retain soil moisture by reducing evaporation, which is especially important during dry periods. Mulch also suppresses weed growth, reducing competition for nutrients and water. Additionally, as organic mulch breaks down, it adds valuable nutrients to the soil, improving soil fertility and structure over time.

When applying mulch, spread a layer about 2 to 3 inches thick around the base of the tree, extending out to the drip line. The drip line is the area directly beneath the outermost branches, where water naturally drips off the tree. It's important to keep the mulch a few inches away from the trunk to prevent rot and discourage pests that might be attracted to the moist environment near the bark. Proper mulching helps create a healthy, thriving environment for the peach tree.

In addition to its practical benefits, mulching also improves the appearance of the garden by providing a neat, finished look around the base of the tree. Organic mulches such as wood chips, straw, or composted leaves blend naturally into the garden landscape, enhancing the overall aesthetic while contributing to the health of the tree. The combination of staking and mulching sets the foundation for a strong, resilient peach tree that can grow and produce fruit successfully in the garden.

Chapter 5

Can I Grow a Peach Tree from a Pit?

Understanding the Process

Growing a peach tree from a pit is a fascinating and rewarding journey, one that offers a unique connection to the natural life cycle of fruit trees. While the process may seem straightforward—planting a seed and watching it grow—it's important to understand that growing a peach tree from a pit involves specific conditions and challenges that differ from other methods of propagation. The journey from pit to tree requires patience, attention to detail, and a bit of luck, but the results can be immensely satisfying for those who embrace the process.

The first aspect to consider when growing a peach tree from a pit is the germination requirements. Peach pits have a tough outer shell that protects the seed inside, and this shell needs to be softened or broken down to allow the seed to sprout. This process, known as stratification, mimics the natural conditions that a peach pit would experience if it were left outdoors over the winter. Stratification involves exposing the pit to cold temperatures for an extended period, typically in a refrigerator, to trigger germination. Without this cold treatment, the seed is unlikely to sprout, making stratification a crucial step in the process.

One of the challenges of growing a peach tree from a pit is the unpredictability of the results. Unlike grafting, which produces a clone of the parent tree, growing from seed introduces genetic variability. This means that the tree that eventually grows from the pit may not produce fruit that is identical to the original peach. The fruit could be smaller, larger, sweeter, or more tart, and in some cases, it may not be as desirable as the parent fruit. However, this variability also adds an element of surprise and excitement, as there is always the possibility of discovering a new and unique variety.

Another key difference between growing a peach tree from a pit and other methods, such as grafting, is the time it takes for the tree to mature and bear fruit. Trees grown from seed typically take longer to reach maturity compared to grafted trees. It may take anywhere from three to seven years before the tree begins to produce fruit, depending on the growing conditions and care provided. This longer timeline requires patience and dedication, but it also allows the gardener to witness the full development of the tree from its earliest stages.

Growing a peach tree from a pit also presents certain challenges related to climate and soil conditions. Peach trees are best suited to temperate climates with cold winters and warm summers. The tree's dormancy period, which is triggered by cold winter temperatures, is essential for the development of healthy fruit. If the climate does not provide enough chill hours during the winter, the tree may struggle to produce fruit. Additionally, peach trees require well-draining soil with a slightly acidic pH to thrive. Ensuring that these conditions are met is critical to the success of growing a peach tree from a pit.

The rewards of growing a peach tree from a pit extend beyond the potential for fruit production. The process itself offers a deep sense of accomplishment and a closer connection to the natural world. Watching a tree grow from a simple pit into a mature, fruit-bearing tree is a testament to the power of nature and the resilience of life. For many gardeners, the journey is just as important as the destination, and the experience of nurturing a peach tree from seed can be a deeply fulfilling endeavor.

Step-by-Step Guide to Planting a Peach Pit

Planting a peach pit is a step-by-step process that begins with selecting a healthy, ripe peach. The pit inside the peach contains the seed, which, with the right care and conditions, can develop into a thriving peach tree. The first step is to carefully extract the pit from the fruit, ensuring that it remains intact. Once the pit is removed, it needs to be cleaned of any remaining fruit pulp. This can be done by rinsing the pit under cold water and gently scrubbing away any residue with a soft brush. It's important to allow the pit to dry for a few days before proceeding with the next steps.

After the pit has dried, the next step is stratification, a process that mimics the natural winter conditions needed to break the seed's dormancy. To stratify the pit, place it in a plastic bag filled with a moist medium, such as sand or peat moss. The bag should then be sealed and placed in the refrigerator for a period of six to twelve weeks. The temperature in the refrigerator should be kept between 34°F and 40°F, as these cold conditions help trigger the germination process. During this time, it's important to check the moisture level of the medium periodically, ensuring it remains damp but not waterlogged.

Once the stratification period is complete, the pit is ready for planting. The first step in planting is to prepare a suitable container or garden bed with well-draining soil. Peach trees prefer slightly acidic soil with a pH between 6.0 and 7.0. If planting in a container, choose one that is at least 12 inches deep to accommodate the growing roots. The pit should be planted about 1 to 2 inches deep, with the pointed end facing downward. Cover the pit with soil and water it thoroughly to settle the soil around the seed. The soil should be kept consistently moist but not soggy, as too much water can cause the pit to rot.

Caring for the seedling as it begins to grow is crucial to its long-term success. Place the container or garden bed in a location that receives full sunlight, as peach trees require at least six to eight hours of direct sunlight each day to thrive. The temperature should be kept warm, ideally between 70°F and 75°F, to encourage germination and growth. As the seedling emerges, continue to water it regularly, keeping the soil moist but not waterlogged. It's also important to protect the young seedling from pests and diseases, which can be particularly harmful during the early stages of growth.

As the seedling grows and develops, it will eventually outgrow its initial container or location. Transplanting the young tree to a larger container or directly into the ground is the next step. When transplanting, choose a location with well-draining soil and plenty of sunlight. Dig a hole that is twice as wide and just as deep as the root ball, and carefully place the seedling in the hole. Fill in the hole with soil, ensuring that the tree is plantcd at the same depth it was in its original container. Water the tree thoroughly after transplanting to help it establish its roots in its new location.

Ongoing care for the young peach tree includes regular watering, fertilization, and pruning. As the tree grows, it will require more water, especially during the hot summer months. Applying a balanced fertilizer in the spring and early summer can help support healthy growth. Pruning should begin in the second or third year to shape the tree and encourage the development of strong, fruit-bearing branches. Protecting the tree from pests and diseases is also important, particularly as it begins to produce fruit.

Following these step-by-step instructions for planting a peach pit will give the seed the best chance of growing into a healthy, productive tree. With the right care and attention, what starts as a simple pit can become a thriving peach tree that provides delicious fruit for years to come.

What to Expect from Your Peach Tree

Growing a peach tree from a pit is a long-term commitment, and understanding what to expect as the tree matures can help gardeners prepare for the various stages of growth and fruit production. The timeline from seedling to a fully mature tree that bears fruit can vary, typically ranging from three to seven years, depending on the growing conditions and care provided. During this time, the tree will go through several distinct phases, each with its own challenges and rewards.

In the first year, the peach tree will focus primarily on establishing its root system and developing its initial structure. During this phase, growth may seem slow, but it's important to remember that the tree is building a strong foundation for future development. Regular watering, proper fertilization, and protection from pests are critical during this time. The tree may produce a few leaves and small branches, but significant growth is usually not visible until the second or third year.

As the tree continues to grow, it will begin to develop more branches and foliage. During this phase, pruning becomes an important task to shape the tree and encourage the growth of strong, productive branches. The goal is to create an open, vase-like structure that allows sunlight and air to reach the interior of the tree. This shape not only supports healthy growth but also helps prevent diseases by improving air circulation. Pruning should be done annually, typically in late winter or early spring, to maintain the tree's shape and promote vigorous growth.

Around the third to fifth year, the tree may begin to produce its first flowers, which is an exciting milestone for any gardener. These blossoms are a sign that the tree is maturing and preparing to produce fruit. However, it's important to manage expectations, as the first few years of fruit production may yield smaller or fewer peaches. The tree is still developing its full fruiting potential, and it may take a few more years before it consistently produces a large, high-quality crop.

One of the unique aspects of growing a peach tree from a pit is the variability in fruit quality and characteristics. Because the tree is grown from seed, the fruit it produces may differ from the original peach in terms of size, flavor, color, and texture. Some trees may produce exceptionally delicious peaches, while others may yield fruit that is less desirable. This variability is a natural part of the process and can be influenced by factors such as soil quality, climate, and care practices. Gardeners should be prepared for the possibility that the fruit may not be identical to the parent peach.

As the tree reaches full maturity, typically around seven years, it should begin to produce a consistent and abundant crop of peaches each year. At this stage, the focus shifts to maintaining the health and productivity of the tree. Regular watering, fertilization, and pruning are essential to support the tree's ongoing growth and fruit production. Thinning the fruit early in the season is also important to ensure that the remaining peaches grow to full size and quality. Proper pest and disease management become increasingly important as the tree ages, as mature trees are more susceptible to certain issues.

Nurturing a peach tree grown from a pit requires patience, dedication, and a willingness to embrace the unknown. The journey from pit to tree is filled with challenges and surprises, but the rewards of growing your own peach tree are well worth the effort. Whether the tree produces a bountiful crop of delicious peaches or simply serves as a beautiful addition to the garden, the experience of growing a peach tree from seed is a deeply fulfilling endeavor.

Chapter 6

Watering and Feeding Your Peach Trees

Watering Essentials

Watering a Peach Tree to Keep It Fresh

Watering is one of the most critical aspects of peach tree care, directly impacting the tree's growth, fruit production, and overall health. Peach trees require consistent moisture, especially during their active growing season, which spans from spring through summer. The key to effective watering is to ensure that the soil remains consistently moist but not waterlogged, as excessive water can lead to root rot and other issues. A well-drained soil is essential to prevent standing water around the tree's roots, which can suffocate the tree and lead to disease.

The frequency and amount of water required by peach trees can vary depending on several factors, including the tree's age, soil type, and climate. Young peach trees, which are still establishing their root systems, need more frequent watering compared to mature trees. During the first year after planting, it's crucial to keep the soil around the young tree consistently moist, watering it deeply once or twice a week. Deep watering encourages the roots to grow downward, helping the tree establish a strong foundation.

Mature peach trees, once established, are more drought-tolerant but still benefit from regular watering, especially during dry spells. These trees typically require about an inch of water per week, either from rainfall or irrigation. The best method for watering mature peach trees is through slow, deep watering techniques, such as drip irrigation or soaker hoses, which deliver water directly to the root zone. This method ensures that the water penetrates deeply into the soil, reaching the roots where it's most needed.

Mulching around the base of the tree helps retain soil moisture and reduce the frequency of watering. A 2 to 3-inch layer of organic mulch, such as wood chips or straw, acts as a barrier against evaporation, keeping the soil cooler and more stable. Mulching also has the added benefit of suppressing weed growth, which can compete with the peach tree for water and nutrients. The combination of proper watering and mulching creates a more favorable environment for the peach tree to thrive.

It's important to monitor the soil moisture regularly, especially during periods of hot, dry weather. Soil moisture can be checked by digging a small hole near the tree's base and feeling the soil with your fingers. If the soil feels dry several inches below the surface, it's time to water. On the other hand, if the soil is consistently wet or soggy, watering should be reduced to prevent waterlogging. Adjusting the watering schedule based on weather conditions and soil moisture levels helps prevent stress and promotes healthy growth.

Overwatering can be just as detrimental as underwatering, leading to issues such as yellowing leaves, root rot, and reduced fruit quality. Signs of overwatering include waterlogged soil, a lack of new growth, and wilting despite the presence of moisture. If these symptoms are observed, it's crucial to reduce the frequency of watering and improve drainage around the tree. Ensuring that the tree receives the right amount of water at the right time is essential for maintaining its health and productivity.

Fertilizing for Growth

Fertilizing is another essential component of peach tree care, providing the nutrients necessary for healthy growth and fruitful production. Peach trees have specific nutritional requirements that must be met to support their vigorous growth and heavy fruit load. Nitrogen, phosphorus, and potassium are the primary macronutrients that peach trees need in significant amounts, but other micronutrients, such as calcium, magnesium, and iron, also play important roles in the tree's overall health.

Nitrogen is the most critical nutrient for peach trees, as it supports vegetative growth, including the development of leaves and shoots. This nutrient is especially important in the early stages of the growing season, when the tree is putting on new growth. However, excessive nitrogen can lead to overly vigorous vegetative growth at the expense of fruit production, so it's important to apply it in the right amounts. A balanced fertilizer with a higher nitrogen content is often recommended during the spring to promote healthy growth.

Phosphorus is essential for root development and flowering, making it crucial for fruit production. Adequate phosphorus levels help ensure that the tree develops a strong root system and produces a healthy bloom, which is the precursor to fruit formation. Phosphorus is typically applied at the time of planting, but it can also be supplemented throughout the growing season as needed. Unlike nitrogen, phosphorus is not as easily leached from the soil, so it's generally applied less frequently.

Potassium, the third macronutrient, plays a key role in fruit quality, helping to improve the size, color, and flavor of the peaches. Potassium also enhances the tree's resistance to diseases and environmental stresses, such as drought or extreme temperatures. A balanced fertilizer that includes potassium is essential during the fruiting stage to ensure that the peaches develop properly and reach their full potential in terms of size and taste.

In addition to these macronutrients, peach trees require several micronutrients to maintain optimal health. Calcium, for example, is important for cell wall structure and fruit firmness, while magnesium is a component of chlorophyll and is essential for photosynthesis. Iron is another important micronutrient that supports chlorophyll production and prevents leaf yellowing, particularly in alkaline soils. Micronutrients are typically applied as part of a complete fertilizer or through foliar sprays if deficiencies are detected.

The timing and method of fertilizer application are crucial to maximizing the benefits. Fertilizer is usually applied in early spring, just as the tree begins to break dormancy and before new growth starts. This timing ensures that the nutrients are available when the tree needs them most. A second application may be made in late spring or early summer, depending on the tree's growth and fruiting stage. Fertilizer can be applied as a granular product spread around the drip line of the tree or as a liquid feed delivered through irrigation.

Over-fertilizing should be avoided, as it can lead to excessive vegetative growth, poor fruit quality, and increased susceptibility to pests and diseases. Symptoms of over-fertilization include dark green, overly lush foliage, delayed fruit ripening, and a lack of fruit production. Regular soil testing can help determine the tree's specific nutrient needs and prevent the application of unnecessary fertilizers. Proper fertilization, based on the tree's growth stage and soil nutrient levels, supports healthy growth and maximizes fruit production.

Organic vs. Chemical Fertilizers

Applying Compost to a Peach Tree as a Natural Fertilizer

Choosing between organic and chemical fertilizers is an important decision that can affect both the health of the peach trees and the surrounding environment. Organic fertilizers are derived from natural sources, such as compost, manure, bone meal, and fish emulsion, and they release nutrients slowly over time as they break down. These fertilizers improve soil structure, increase microbial activity, and provide a steady, long-term supply of nutrients. Organic fertilizers are often favored by gardeners who prioritize sustainability and soil health.

One of the main benefits of organic fertilizers is their ability to improve soil fertility beyond just supplying nutrients. Organic matter in these fertilizers enhances soil texture, increases water retention, and promotes the growth of beneficial soil organisms, such as earthworms and microbes. These organisms help break down organic matter into usable nutrients and contribute to the overall health of the soil ecosystem. Over time, the use of organic fertilizers can lead to healthier, more resilient soil, which supports the long-term growth of peach trees.

Organic fertilizers also pose less risk of nutrient runoff and environmental pollution compared to chemical fertilizers. Because they release nutrients slowly and gradually, there is less chance of over-fertilization or nutrient leaching into groundwater. This makes organic fertilizers a more environmentally friendly option, particularly in areas where water quality is a concern. The slow-release nature of organic fertilizers also means that they are less likely to burn plant roots or cause other damage associated with rapid nutrient release.

On the other hand, chemical fertilizers are formulated to deliver nutrients in a highly concentrated and readily available form. These fertilizers can provide an immediate boost to peach trees, especially if a specific nutrient deficiency is identified. Chemical fertilizers are often easier to apply and are available in precise formulations that allow for targeted feeding based on the tree's needs. For gardeners looking for quick results or those managing large orchards, chemical fertilizers can be an efficient way to meet the nutritional demands of peach trees.

However, chemical fertilizers come with certain drawbacks. They can lead to soil degradation over time if used exclusively, as they do not contribute organic matter or improve soil structure. Repeated use of chemical fertilizers can also disrupt the balance of soil microorganisms, potentially leading to a decline in soil health. Additionally, the high solubility of chemical fertilizers means that they are more prone to leaching and runoff, which can contribute to water pollution and harm aquatic ecosystems.

When using chemical fertilizers, it's important to follow application instructions carefully to avoid over-fertilization. Applying too much can lead to nutrient imbalances, which can harm the peach tree and reduce fruit quality. Chemical fertilizers should be applied based on the results of a soil test to ensure that they are addressing specific nutrient needs rather than being applied indiscriminately. Responsible use of chemical fertilizers can support healthy peach tree growth without causing undue harm to the environment.

The choice between organic and chemical fertilizers depends on the gardener's goals, values, and the specific needs of the peach trees. Some gardeners may choose to use a combination of both, applying organic fertilizers to improve soil health and using chemical fertilizers for targeted nutrient supplementation. Understanding the benefits and limitations of each type allows for informed decision-making that supports both the immediate and long-term health of the peach trees.

Chapter 7

Pruning Your Peach Trees

The Importance of Pruning

Pruning Peach Tree

Pruning is an essential practice in peach tree care, playing a pivotal role in maintaining the health, structure, and productivity of the tree. Regular pruning helps to remove dead, diseased, or damaged wood, preventing the spread of pests and diseases that can compromise the tree's vitality. By removing these unhealthy parts, the tree can direct its energy toward producing new, healthy growth, leading to a more robust and productive tree. Pruning also improves air circulation within the canopy, reducing the likelihood of fungal diseases, which thrive in moist, stagnant conditions.

Another critical reason for pruning peach trees is to manage the tree's size and shape. Peach trees can grow quite vigorously, and without regular pruning, they can become overgrown and unmanageable. Pruning helps to maintain a desirable tree structure, with a balanced canopy that allows sunlight to penetrate all parts of the tree. This exposure to sunlight is crucial for fruit ripening, as peaches need ample sunlight to develop their characteristic sweetness and color. A well-pruned tree also makes it easier to harvest the fruit, as the branches are kept at a manageable height.

Pruning also plays a key role in promoting fruit production. Peach trees produce fruit on one-year-old wood, meaning that the branches that grew the previous year will bear fruit in the current year. Regular pruning encourages the growth of new shoots, which are essential for next year's fruit production. By selectively removing older, unproductive wood, pruning stimulates the development of new fruiting branches, ensuring a continuous supply of peaches each season. Without pruning, the tree can become crowded with old wood, leading to a decline in fruit production over time.

The timing of pruning is crucial to achieving the best results. The ideal time to prune peach trees is in late winter or early spring, just before the buds begin to swell. Pruning during this period allows the tree to recover quickly as it enters the active growing season. It's important to avoid pruning during late fall or early winter, as this can stimulate new growth that is vulnerable to frost damage. Proper timing helps to minimize stress on the tree and maximizes the benefits of pruning.

In addition to improving tree health and fruit production, pruning also helps to prevent structural issues. Peach trees can be prone to developing weak or poorly angled branches, which are more likely to break under the weight of a heavy fruit load or in strong winds. Pruning helps to remove these weak branches and encourages the growth of strong, well-angled branches that can support a bountiful harvest. A well-pruned tree is more resilient and less likely to suffer damage from environmental stresses.

Pruning is not just about cutting back growth; it's about shaping the tree in a way that promotes its long-term health and productivity. Each cut made during pruning has a purpose, whether it's to remove unhealthy wood, encourage new growth, or improve the tree's structure. Understanding the reasons behind each cut allows for more effective pruning, leading to a healthier and more productive peach tree.

Pruning Techniques

Pruning peach trees requires a combination of art and science, with specific techniques that vary depending on the age, size, and overall health of the tree. One of the most common and effective pruning techniques for peach trees is the open-center or vase shape, which involves creating a tree structure with an open center and outward-facing branches. This shape allows maximum sunlight penetration and air circulation, both of which are essential for healthy fruit development and disease prevention. The open-center shape is particularly well-suited for peach trees, as it promotes the growth of strong, well-spaced branches that can support heavy fruit loads.

To achieve the open-center shape, the pruning process begins early in the tree's life. In the first year after planting, select three to four strong, well-spaced branches to serve as the main scaffold branches. These branches should be evenly distributed around the tree and angled outward, away from the center. The central leader, or main vertical stem, is then removed just above the highest scaffold branch, which encourages the tree to develop a broad, open canopy. This initial pruning sets the foundation for the tree's future structure and growth.

As the tree matures, annual pruning focuses on maintaining the open-center shape and removing any branches that disrupt this structure. This includes removing any inward-growing branches, which can crowd the center of the tree and block sunlight. Additionally, any branches that cross or rub against each other should be pruned to prevent damage and disease. The goal is to create a balanced canopy with evenly spaced branches that allow light and air to reach all parts of the tree.

Another important pruning technique is thinning, which involves selectively removing some of the fruiting wood to prevent overcrowding and improve fruit quality. Peach trees can produce an abundance of fruit, but if left unthinned, the fruit may be small and of poor quality. Thinning helps to reduce the number of fruiting branches, allowing the remaining branches to produce larger, better-quality peaches. Thinning also prevents the tree from becoming overloaded with fruit, which can lead to broken branches and stress on the tree.

Heading cuts are another technique used in pruning peach trees. A heading cut involves shortening a branch to a bud or lateral branch, which encourages the growth of new shoots. This technique is often used to control the height of the tree and to stimulate the growth of new fruiting wood. Heading cuts should be made just above a healthy bud, which will produce new growth in the desired direction. Care should be taken to avoid making heading cuts too close to the bud, as this can damage the bud and prevent new growth.

It's also important to remove any suckers and water sprouts during the pruning process. Suckers are shoots that grow from the base of the tree or the rootstock, while water sprouts are vigorous, upright shoots that grow from the trunk or main branches. Both suckers and water sprouts can divert energy away from the fruiting branches and should be removed to maintain the tree's health and productivity. Removing these unwanted shoots helps to direct the tree's energy toward producing fruit rather than unnecessary growth.

The use of proper tools is essential for effective pruning. Sharp, clean pruning shears, loppers, and saws should be used to make clean cuts that heal quickly and reduce the risk of disease. It's also important to disinfect pruning tools between cuts, especially when working on diseased wood, to prevent the spread of pathogens. Investing in quality tools and maintaining them properly ensures that the pruning process is efficient and beneficial to the tree.

Mastering the techniques of pruning peach trees is key to ensuring a healthy, productive tree. Each technique, from thinning to heading cuts, plays a specific role in shaping the tree and promoting its growth. With the right approach, pruning becomes a powerful tool in maximizing fruit production and maintaining the long-term health of the peach tree.

Training Young Trees

Training young peach trees is a critical aspect of ensuring their future health, structure, and productivity. The training process begins in the first year after planting and continues through the early years of the tree's life. The primary goal of training is to establish a strong, well-balanced framework of branches that will support the tree's growth and fruit production for years to come. Training is different from pruning in that it involves guiding the tree's growth through strategic pruning cuts and the use of supports or ties, rather than simply removing unwanted growth.

The first step in training a young peach tree is to select the main scaffold branches that will form the tree's structure. These branches should be chosen in the first year after planting when the tree is still young and flexible. Typically, three to four strong, well-spaced branches are selected to become the primary scaffold branches. These branches should be evenly distributed around the trunk and angled outward at a 45 to 60-degree angle. This angle provides the best balance of strength and flexibility, allowing the branches to support heavy fruit loads without breaking.

Once the scaffold branches are selected, the central leader (the main vertical stem) is pruned back to just above the highest scaffold branch. This encourages the tree to develop an open-center or vase shape, which is ideal for peach trees. The open-center shape allows maximum sunlight to reach all parts of the tree, which is essential for fruit ripening and overall tree health. As the tree grows, it's important to continue training it to maintain this shape, removing any inward-growing branches or shoots that could crowd the center of the tree.

In addition to selecting and training scaffold branches, it's important to manage the growth of lateral branches on the scaffold limbs. Lateral branches should be spaced evenly along the length of the scaffold branches, with no two laterals growing from the same point. This spacing prevents overcrowding and allows each branch to receive adequate sunlight and air circulation. If necessary, lateral branches can be pruned or tied to guide their growth in the desired direction, helping to maintain the tree's structure.

As the tree matures, it's important to monitor the angle at which the branches grow. Branches that grow at too narrow an angle from the trunk are more likely to break under the weight of fruit. If a scaffold branch is growing at too narrow an angle, it can be gently pulled outward and secured with a soft tie to encourage it to grow at a wider angle. This technique helps to strengthen the branch and reduce the risk of breakage in the future. Regularly checking the angles of the branches and making adjustments as needed is a key part of training young peach trees.

Training also involves managing the tree's height to ensure that it remains accessible for maintenance and harvesting. If the tree begins to grow too tall, the central leader can be pruned back to a lateral branch to encourage outward rather than upward growth. This not only keeps the tree at a manageable height but also promotes the development of a wider, more productive canopy. Maintaining the right balance between height and spread is crucial for a well-trained peach tree.

The use of supports and ties can be helpful in training young trees, especially in windy areas or when branches need to be guided into the desired position. Soft, flexible ties should be used to avoid damaging the bark or constricting the branch as it grows. These ties can be adjusted as the tree grows to ensure that the branches continue to develop in the desired direction. Using the right supports and ties helps to shape the tree during its early years, leading to a stronger and more resilient structure.

Chapter 8

Protecting Peach Trees from Pests and Diseases

Common Peach Tree Pests

Peach trees are susceptible to a variety of pests that can significantly impact their health and fruit production. One of the most common and destructive pests is the peach tree borer, a type of moth whose larvae burrow into the tree's trunk and feed on the inner bark. This damage can weaken the tree, reduce its vigor, and even lead to death if the infestation is severe. Signs of a peach tree borer infestation include gumming (a sticky sap-like substance) around the base of the tree and sawdust-like frass (excrement) near the entry holes. Managing peach tree borers involves careful monitoring, applying protective insecticides if necessary, and maintaining tree health to improve resistance.

Another frequent pest is the aphid, a small, soft-bodied insect that feeds on the sap of peach tree leaves and young shoots. Aphid infestations can cause leaves to curl, yellow, and drop prematurely, weakening the tree and reducing its ability to photosynthesize. Additionally, aphids excrete honeydew, a sticky substance that can lead to the growth of sooty mold on leaves and fruit. Effective control of aphids includes encouraging natural predators such as ladybugs, using insecticidal soaps, and employing cultural practices like pruning to remove infested shoots.

Oriental fruit moths are another serious threat to peach trees. The larvae of these moths tunnel into shoots and fruits, causing wilting and internal damage. Infested fruit often ripens prematurely and falls from the tree, reducing the overall yield. Monitoring for the presence of adult moths through pheromone traps and applying appropriate insecticides during the moths' egg-laying period can help control this pest. Regular inspection of fruit and shoots for signs of infestation is also critical in managing oriental fruit moths.

Scale insects, including the San Jose scale, can be particularly problematic for peach trees. These pests attach themselves to the bark, leaves, and fruit, sucking sap from the tree and causing yellowing, reduced vigor, and sometimes branch dieback. Severe infestations can lead to significant tree decline and loss of fruit production. Control of scale insects typically involves the application of horticultural oils during the dormant season, which smother the scales and prevent them from feeding. Additionally, maintaining tree health through proper fertilization and watering can reduce the impact of scale infestations.

Another common pest is the plum curculio, a small beetle that lays its eggs in developing peach fruit. The larvae then burrow into the fruit, causing it to become misshapen, scarred, and eventually drop from the tree. This pest is particularly challenging to control because it affects the fruit directly, leading to significant losses if not managed effectively. Monitoring for adult beetles and applying insecticides at the appropriate time, along with removing and destroying infested fruit, are essential steps in controlling plum curculio.

Spider mites, though small, can cause significant damage to peach trees, particularly during hot, dry weather. These tiny arachnids feed on the undersides of leaves, causing stippling, bronzing, and eventual leaf drop. Severe infestations can weaken the tree and reduce fruit quality. Regular monitoring, maintaining proper irrigation to reduce plant stress, and using miticides when necessary are effective strategies for managing spider mites. Encouraging natural predators, such as predatory mites, can also help keep spider mite populations in check.

Protecting peach trees from these common pests requires a proactive approach that includes regular monitoring, timely interventions, and maintaining overall tree health. Understanding the lifecycle and habits of these pests enables better management and helps prevent infestations from becoming severe.

Preventing Diseases

Peach trees are vulnerable to a range of diseases that can affect their growth, fruit production, and longevity. One of the most notorious diseases is peach leaf curl, caused by the fungus *Taphrina deformans*. This disease leads to distorted, thickened, and discolored leaves, which eventually drop from the tree. The loss of leaves weakens the tree, reducing its ability to photosynthesize and produce fruit. Preventing peach leaf curl involves applying a fungicide spray during the dormant season, typically in late fall or early winter. Choosing resistant peach varieties and maintaining good air circulation around the tree can also reduce the risk of infection.

Brown rot is another common and destructive disease that affects peach trees. Caused by the fungus *Monilinia fructicola*, brown rot can infect blossoms, shoots, and fruit, leading to wilting, fruit rot, and significant yield losses. Infected fruit develop brown, fuzzy spores and eventually mummify, spreading the disease further if left on the tree. To prevent brown rot, it's important to prune the tree regularly to improve air circulation, remove and destroy any infected fruit or plant material, and apply fungicides during the bloom period and just before harvest.

Bacterial spot, caused by the bacterium *Xanthomonas campestris pv. pruni*, is another serious disease that can affect both the leaves and fruit of peach trees. Symptoms include small, dark lesions on leaves, which may lead to premature leaf drop, as well as water-soaked spots on fruit that become sunken and cracked. Preventing bacterial spot involves selecting resistant varieties, applying copper-based bactericides during the growing season, and practicing good sanitation by removing and destroying affected plant material.

Cytospora canker, a fungal disease caused by *Cytospora spp.*, can be particularly devastating for peach trees, leading to branch dieback and potentially killing the tree if not managed. The fungus enters the tree through wounds or pruning cuts, causing sunken, discolored areas on the bark that ooze amber-colored gum. To prevent cytospora canker, it's crucial to avoid unnecessary wounding of the tree, prune during dry weather to reduce the risk of infection, and apply protective fungicides if necessary. Maintaining tree vigor through proper fertilization and watering can also help the tree resist infection.

Peach scab, caused by the fungus *Cladosporium carpophilum*, primarily affects the fruit, leading to small, dark spots that can make the fruit unmarketable. While peach scab is generally less severe than other diseases, it can still impact fruit quality and yield. Preventing peach scab involves applying fungicide sprays during the early stages of fruit development, particularly in wet or humid conditions that favor the spread of the fungus. Pruning to improve air circulation and sunlight penetration can also help reduce the incidence of scab.

Phytophthora root rot is a soil-borne disease caused by *Phytophthora spp.*, which can be devastating to peach trees, particularly in poorly drained soils. The disease causes the roots to rot, leading to yellowing leaves, wilting, and eventual tree death. Preventing phytophthora root rot involves ensuring that the tree is planted in well-drained soil, avoiding overwatering, and applying fungicides to the soil if necessary. In areas with a history of phytophthora, choosing resistant rootstocks can help reduce the risk of infection.

Preventing these diseases requires a combination of good cultural practices, timely fungicide applications, and vigilant monitoring. Keeping the trees healthy and minimizing environmental stress can go a long way in reducing the susceptibility of peach trees to these diseases.

Organic Pest Control Options

Organic pest control methods offer a sustainable and environmentally friendly approach to managing pests on peach trees. These methods rely on natural predators, biological controls, and organic substances to keep pest populations in check without the use of synthetic chemicals. One of the most effective organic pest control strategies is the introduction or encouragement of beneficial insects that prey on common peach tree pests. For example, ladybugs and lacewings are natural predators of aphids, while parasitic wasps can help control scale insects and caterpillars. Creating a garden environment that attracts these beneficial insects, such as planting flowering plants that provide nectar and pollen, can enhance their presence and effectiveness.

Neem oil is a widely used organic pesticide that is effective against a variety of peach tree pests, including aphids, mites, and scale insects. Derived from the seeds of the neem tree, neem oil acts as an insect growth regulator, disrupting the life cycle of pests and preventing them from feeding, molting, or reproducing. Neem oil is biodegradable and has low toxicity to humans, pets, and beneficial insects, making it a safe option for organic gardening. It's important to apply neem oil during the early morning or late evening to avoid harming pollinators like bees, which are active during the day.

Horticultural oils, such as dormant oil and summer oil, are another effective organic option for controlling pests on peach trees. These oils work by smothering pests, including scale insects, mites, and overwintering eggs, preventing them from breathing. Dormant oil is applied during the tree's dormant season, typically in late winter, while summer oil can be applied during the growing season. Horticultural oils are safe for the environment and do not leave harmful residues, making them an excellent choice for organic pest control.

Insecticidal soaps are another tool in the organic gardener's arsenal, particularly for soft-bodied pests like aphids and spider mites. These soaps work by breaking down the outer protective layer of the pests, causing them to dehydrate and die. Insecticidal soaps are effective when applied directly to the pests and are generally safe for humans, animals, and beneficial insects. However, care should be taken to avoid applying insecticidal soaps during hot weather or direct sunlight, as this can cause leaf burn on the peach trees.

Companion planting is a cultural practice that can help deter pests from peach trees while promoting a healthier garden ecosystem. Certain plants, such as marigolds, garlic, and nasturtiums, have natural pest-repellent properties and can be planted near peach trees to discourage pests like aphids and nematodes. Additionally, planting a diverse range of plants can attract beneficial insects and reduce the likelihood of pest outbreaks. Companion planting not only helps with pest control but also contributes to overall garden health and biodiversity.

Traps and barriers are physical methods of organic pest control that can help protect peach trees from specific pests. Pheromone traps, for example, can be used to monitor and reduce populations of moths like the oriental fruit moth. Sticky traps can be placed around the tree to catch crawling insects like ants and aphids. Barriers such as tree wraps or trunk guards can prevent pests like borers from accessing the tree's trunk and causing damage. These physical controls are effective and environmentally friendly options for managing pests.

Chapter 9

Managing Peach Tree Problems

Dealing with Frost and Cold

Peach trees are particularly vulnerable to frost and cold temperatures, especially during the early spring when buds and blossoms are developing. Frost can cause significant damage to peach trees, leading to the loss of blossoms and young fruit, which in turn reduces the overall yield. One of the most effective ways to protect peach trees from frost is through site selection. Planting peach trees on a slope or in a location that allows cold air to drain away can help reduce the risk of frost damage. Avoiding low-lying areas where cold air tends to settle is key in minimizing frost exposure.

In addition to site selection, monitoring weather conditions closely during the spring is essential for frost protection. When a frost warning is issued, there are several methods to protect the trees. One common approach is to use frost blankets or covers to insulate the trees and keep the blossoms warm. These covers should be applied in the evening before temperatures drop and removed in the morning once the sun is up and temperatures have risen. For smaller trees, individual covers can be used, while larger trees may require larger, specially designed frost cloths.

Another method to protect peach trees from frost is through the use of water. Spraying the trees with water before a frost can create a protective layer of ice that insulates the blossoms and prevents them from freezing.

This method works because the water releases latent heat as it freezes, helping to keep the temperature around the blossoms just above freezing. However, this technique requires precise timing and careful management to avoid damaging the tree with excessive ice buildup.

Heaters or wind machines can also be employed to protect peach trees from frost. Heaters placed strategically around the orchard can raise the temperature enough to prevent frost from forming. Wind machines, on the other hand, work by mixing the warmer air above with the cooler air near the ground, raising the overall temperature around the trees. Both methods can be effective but may require significant investment and are typically used in commercial orchards rather than home gardens.

Winter protection for peach trees involves more than just preventing frost damage. In regions with harsh winters, it's important to protect the tree's trunk and roots from extreme cold. Applying a thick layer of mulch around the base of the tree helps insulate the roots and protect them from freezing temperatures. Wrapping the trunk with burlap or tree wrap can prevent sunscald and frost cracks, which occur when the trunk warms up during the day and then rapidly cools at night. These protective measures are essential for maintaining the tree's health during the winter months.

Pruning also plays a role in frost protection. Late winter or early spring pruning should be done with care to avoid stimulating new growth that could be damaged by a late frost. Delaying pruning until after the risk of frost has passed can help protect the tree's buds and blossoms. Additionally, pruning to create an open-center shape improves air circulation and allows sunlight to reach all parts of the tree, reducing the risk of frost damage.

Troubleshooting Growth Issues

Peach trees, like all plants, can encounter various growth issues that may impact their health and fruit production. Identifying and addressing these problems early is crucial to maintaining a thriving tree. One common growth issue is poor or stunted growth, which can result from a variety of factors, including inadequate sunlight, poor soil conditions, or insufficient watering. Ensuring that the tree receives at least six to eight hours of direct sunlight each day and that the soil is well-drained and nutrient-rich can help promote healthy growth. If poor growth persists, a soil test may be necessary to identify nutrient deficiencies or imbalances.

Another issue that peach trees may face is leaf yellowing, which can be a sign of several underlying problems. Chlorosis, a condition where the leaves turn yellow due to a lack of chlorophyll, is often caused by iron deficiency, particularly in alkaline soils. This can be addressed by applying chelated iron to the soil or as a foliar spray. Leaf yellowing can also result from overwatering, which causes root rot and limits the tree's ability to absorb nutrients. Adjusting the watering schedule and improving soil drainage can help resolve this issue.

Premature leaf drop is another growth problem that can affect peach trees. This issue can be caused by environmental stress, such as drought, extreme temperatures, or nutrient deficiencies. Pests and diseases can also lead to premature leaf drop. Regular monitoring for signs of pest infestations or diseases, such as leaf spots or lesions, is essential for identifying the cause of leaf drop. Implementing proper cultural practices, such as mulching to retain soil moisture and applying balanced fertilizers, can help reduce stress and prevent premature leaf drop.

Peach trees may also experience poor fruit set or fruit drop, where the tree produces few fruits or the fruits drop before they mature. This issue can be due to several factors, including inadequate pollination, poor weather conditions during bloom, or nutrient imbalances. Ensuring that the tree is planted in a location with good air circulation and is accessible to pollinators can improve fruit set. Applying fertilizers rich in phosphorus and potassium during the bloom period can also support fruit development. If poor fruit set persists, thinning the fruit can help the tree focus its energy on producing fewer but larger and healthier peaches.

Weak or spindly branches are another common growth issue in peach trees. These branches are often the result of overcrowding, poor pruning practices, or excessive nitrogen fertilization, which promotes vegetative growth at the expense of fruit production. Regular pruning to remove overcrowded or poorly angled branches helps strengthen the tree's structure. Avoiding excessive nitrogen applications during the growing season can also prevent the development of weak branches. Encouraging a balanced nutrient regimen supports the overall health and structure of the tree.

Another growth issue that peach trees may encounter is the development of suckers and water sprouts. Suckers are vigorous shoots that grow from the base of the tree or rootstock, while water sprouts are upright shoots that emerge from the trunk or branches. Both types of growth can divert energy from the main tree and should be removed as soon as they appear. Regularly inspecting the tree and promptly removing suckers and water sprouts helps direct the tree's energy toward producing healthy fruiting wood.

Handling Nutrient Deficiencies

Nutrient deficiencies in peach trees can lead to a variety of symptoms, including poor growth, leaf discoloration, and reduced fruit production. Identifying and addressing these deficiencies is essential for maintaining the health and productivity of the tree. One of the most common nutrient deficiencies in peach trees is nitrogen deficiency, which manifests as pale green or yellow leaves and reduced vegetative growth. Nitrogen is a critical nutrient for promoting healthy foliage and overall tree vigor. Addressing nitrogen deficiency typically involves applying a balanced fertilizer that is rich in nitrogen during the early growing season.

Phosphorus deficiency is another issue that can affect peach trees, particularly in soils that are low in organic matter or have a high pH. Symptoms of phosphorus deficiency include dark green or purplish leaves, stunted growth, and poor fruit set. Phosphorus is essential for root development and flowering, making it a crucial nutrient for fruit-bearing trees. Applying a phosphorus-rich fertilizer, such as bone meal or rock phosphate, can help correct this deficiency. Ensuring that the soil pH is within the optimal range for phosphorus availability (around 6.0 to 7.0) is also important for preventing this issue.

Potassium deficiency can lead to weak branches, small or poorly colored fruit, and leaf scorching, particularly along the edges. Potassium plays a key role in water regulation, enzyme activation, and overall plant resilience. Trees that are deficient in potassium may be more susceptible to drought stress and disease. To address potassium deficiency, a fertilizer containing potassium, such as potassium sulfate or wood ash, can be applied. Potassium is also important for fruit quality, so ensuring adequate levels is critical during the fruiting period.

Calcium deficiency, although less common, can cause significant problems for peach trees, including blossom-end rot in the fruit and dieback of new growth. Calcium is important for cell wall formation and stability, and a deficiency can lead to weakened tissue and increased susceptibility to disease. Calcium deficiency is often related to irregular watering or competition with other nutrients like potassium. Applying lime to raise soil pH or gypsum to add calcium without affecting pH can help address this deficiency. Regular watering to maintain consistent soil moisture also supports calcium uptake.

Magnesium deficiency is another nutrient issue that can affect peach trees, leading to interveinal chlorosis (yellowing between the veins) on older leaves. Magnesium is a central component of chlorophyll, the molecule responsible for photosynthesis. A lack of magnesium can reduce the tree's ability to produce energy, leading to reduced growth and fruit production. Epsom salts (magnesium sulfate) can be applied to the soil or as a foliar spray to correct magnesium deficiency. Ensuring that the soil is not overly acidic, which can limit magnesium availability, is also important.

Iron deficiency, often referred to as iron chlorosis, is a common problem in peach trees growing in alkaline soils. Symptoms include yellowing of young leaves with green veins, leading to reduced growth and vigor. Iron is essential for chlorophyll production, and its deficiency can severely impact the tree's ability to photosynthesize. Iron chelates, which are more readily available to plants, can be applied to the soil or as a foliar spray to address iron deficiency. Lowering soil pH through the addition of sulfur or organic matter can also help improve iron availability.

Chapter 10

The Art of Thinning Peaches

Why Thinning Matters

Thinning peaches is a crucial practice that directly impacts the quality of the fruit and the overall health of the peach tree. When a peach tree is left to set all of its fruit, the sheer number of peaches can overwhelm the tree, leading to smaller, less flavorful fruit. This is because the tree's energy and nutrients are divided among too many fruits, reducing the size and sweetness of each peach. Thinning helps to balance the fruit load, allowing the remaining peaches to grow larger, develop better flavor, and achieve a more desirable texture.

In addition to improving fruit quality, thinning also reduces the risk of branch breakage. Peach trees can produce an abundance of fruit, and if all of this fruit is allowed to mature, the combined weight can cause branches to snap, especially during windy or rainy conditions. By removing excess fruit early in the season, the strain on the branches is reduced, helping to prevent damage and ensuring that the tree remains structurally sound. This is particularly important for young trees that are still developing their framework and may not have the strength to support a heavy crop.

Thinning is also important for maintaining the health of the tree. Overloaded trees are more susceptible to stress, which can weaken the tree and make it more vulnerable to pests and diseases. When a tree is stressed, it may also produce fewer flowers the following year, leading to a reduced crop. By thinning the fruit, the tree can focus its resources on producing a healthy crop without compromising its long-term vitality. This practice contributes to the overall sustainability of the tree, ensuring that it remains productive for many years.

Moreover, thinning helps to promote uniform ripening of the fruit. When peaches are spaced too closely together, they can shade each other, leading to uneven ripening. This results in some peaches being overripe while others are still underdeveloped. Thinning creates more space between the remaining fruits, allowing them to receive adequate sunlight and air circulation. This exposure to sunlight is crucial for the development of sugars, which contribute to the peach's sweetness and flavor. Uniform ripening also makes harvesting easier, as the fruit will mature at a more consistent rate.

The practice of thinning is not only about improving the current season's crop but also about ensuring the future productivity of the tree. When a tree is allowed to overproduce one year, it can lead to a phenomenon known as biennial bearing, where the tree alternates between heavy and light crops each year. This irregularity can be problematic for growers who rely on consistent yields. Thinning helps to moderate the tree's output, reducing the likelihood of biennial bearing and promoting a more regular fruiting cycle.

Thinning also plays a role in enhancing the marketability of the fruit. Larger, well-formed peaches are more attractive to consumers and can command higher prices in the market. For home gardeners, thinning means more satisfying harvests, with peaches that are not only delicious but also visually appealing. The practice of thinning is an investment in quality, leading to a more rewarding experience for both commercial growers and home gardeners.

How and When to Thin

The process of thinning peaches involves the careful removal of excess fruit from the tree to ensure that the remaining peaches can develop to their full potential. Timing is critical when it comes to thinning, as the practice must be done early enough in the season to influence fruit development, but not so early that it disrupts the natural fruit drop that occurs after bloom. The best time to thin peaches is typically three to four weeks after the petals have fallen, during what is known as the "shuck split" stage. At this point, the young fruit is about the size of a nickel, making it easier to assess and remove excess fruit.

Before beginning the thinning process, it's important to have a clear understanding of the desired fruit spacing. For most peach varieties, the ideal spacing between fruits is about 6 to 8 inches. This spacing allows each peach enough room to grow and receive adequate sunlight and air circulation. When thinning, aim to leave the healthiest, most robust fruit on the tree while removing smaller, misshapen, or damaged peaches. This selective removal ensures that the remaining fruit has the best chance of developing into high-quality peaches.

Thinning can be done by hand, which allows for precise control over which fruits are removed. To thin by hand, gently grasp the fruit between your thumb and forefinger and twist it off the branch. It's important to avoid pulling the fruit, as this can damage the stem or nearby fruits. Hand thinning is the most common method and is especially useful for small orchards or home gardens where individual attention to each tree is feasible. In larger commercial operations, mechanical thinning methods may be used, but hand thinning is still preferred for its accuracy.

Another method of thinning is the use of specialized pruning shears or clippers, which can be particularly helpful for reaching higher branches or for removing larger clusters of fruit. When using tools to thin, it's important to disinfect the blades regularly to prevent the spread of disease between trees. The use of tools can make the thinning process more efficient, especially in larger trees or orchards where time is a factor. Whether thinning by hand or with tools, the goal is to create even spacing between the remaining fruits to ensure optimal growth.

In some cases, chemical thinners may be used to reduce the labor involved in hand thinning. These chemicals, when applied at the right time, can cause the tree to naturally drop a portion of its fruit. However, the use of chemical thinners requires careful calibration, as over-application can result in excessive fruit drop, while under-application may have little effect. Chemical thinning is typically used in large-scale commercial operations where hand thinning is not practical, but it requires a thorough understanding of the specific tree variety and local growing conditions to be effective.

The weather conditions during thinning can also influence the process. Thinning is best done during dry weather to reduce the risk of spreading diseases such as brown rot. Wet or humid conditions can create a favorable environment for fungal infections, so it's important to avoid thinning during or immediately after rain. Choosing a dry, sunny day for thinning helps to minimize the risk of disease and ensures that the tree is in optimal condition for the process.

Common Mistakes to Avoid

Thinning peaches is an art that requires attention to detail and an understanding of the tree's growth habits. However, even experienced growers can make mistakes during the thinning process that can impact the quality of the fruit and the health of the tree. One common mistake is thinning too early or too late in the season. Thinning too early, before the natural fruit drop has occurred, can result in removing fruit that the tree would naturally shed, leading to an unnecessary reduction in the crop. Thinning too late, on the other hand, can limit the effectiveness of the practice, as the remaining fruit may not have enough time to benefit from the increased resources.

Another mistake is leaving too many fruits on the tree after thinning. It can be tempting to leave more fruits on the tree in the hopes of a larger harvest, but this often results in smaller, lower-quality peaches. The tree's resources are finite, and when spread too thin, they cannot adequately support the development of large, flavorful fruit. It's important to adhere to the recommended spacing of 6 to 8 inches between fruits to ensure that each peach receives enough nutrients and sunlight. Overcrowding can also increase the risk of disease, as closely packed fruits can trap moisture and create a breeding ground for pathogens.

Improper technique during thinning is another common issue. Pulling or tugging at the fruit can damage the branches or neighboring fruits, leading to wounds that may become entry points for pests and diseases. It's important to use a gentle twisting motion when removing the fruit, and to ensure that only the intended fruit is removed. If using tools such as pruning shears, care must be taken to avoid cutting into the branches or leaving behind stubs that can harbor infections. Clean, precise cuts are essential for maintaining the tree's health during thinning.

Failing to monitor weather conditions before thinning is a mistake that can have serious consequences. Thinning during wet or humid weather can increase the risk of spreading diseases, particularly fungal infections like brown rot. These conditions create an ideal environment for pathogens, which can quickly spread through the tree if the thinning process creates wounds or exposes the fruit to moisture. Choosing a dry, sunny day for thinning helps to reduce the risk of disease and ensures that the tree remains healthy after the process.

Another mistake to avoid is neglecting to thin the tree at all. Some growers may skip thinning in the hopes of maximizing their harvest, but this often leads to poor results. Without thinning, the tree may produce a large number of small, subpar fruits, and the added weight can cause branches to break. In the long term, failing to thin can also stress the tree, reducing its overall vigor and leading to a cycle of biennial bearing, where the tree produces heavy crops one year and light crops the next. Regular thinning is essential for maintaining consistent, high-quality harvests.

Over-reliance on chemical thinners is another potential pitfall. While chemical thinning can be effective in reducing the labor involved in hand thinning, it requires careful management to avoid over-thinning or under-thinning. The application of chemical thinners must be timed precisely, and the concentration must be carefully controlled based on the specific variety and local growing conditions. Misapplication can result in excessive fruit drop or uneven thinning, which can negatively impact the crop. For this reason, many growers prefer hand thinning or use chemical thinners in combination with hand thinning for greater control.

Chapter 11

Harvesting Your Peaches

When to Harvest

Harvest peaches at peak ripeness for optimal flavor and texture

Timing is everything when it comes to harvesting peaches, as picking the fruit at the right stage of ripeness is crucial for achieving the best flavor and texture. Peaches do not continue to ripen significantly after being picked, so it's important to harvest them at their peak. The first indication that peaches are ready to be harvested is a change in color. The background color of the fruit, which is the area of the skin not exposed to direct sunlight, should turn from green to a yellow or creamy color, depending on the variety. The fruit's size and shape should also be fully developed, with a slight give when gently pressed.

In addition to visual cues, the taste and aroma of the peaches are important indicators of ripeness. A ripe peach will have a sweet, fragrant aroma that is noticeable even from a distance. If the peach lacks this aroma or has a green, grassy smell, it's likely not ready to be harvested. Tasting a few peaches before harvesting the entire crop can also help determine if they have reached the desired level of sweetness and flavor. If the fruit tastes tart or lacks juiciness, it may need more time on the tree.

The timing of the harvest can vary depending on the variety of peach and the growing conditions. Early-season varieties may be ready for harvest as early as May or June, while late-season varieties may not be ready until August or September. It's important to monitor the fruit closely as it approaches maturity, as peaches can ripen quickly once they reach a certain stage. Harvesting too early can result in fruit that is hard and lacks flavor, while waiting too long can lead to overripe fruit that is prone to bruising and spoilage.

Another factor to consider when determining the best time to harvest peaches is the intended use of the fruit. Peaches that will be eaten fresh should be harvested at full ripeness when the flavor and texture are at their peak. For peaches that will be canned, frozen, or used in cooking, it may be better to pick them slightly earlier, when they are firm but fully colored. This ensures that the fruit holds up better during processing and retains its flavor and texture.

Weather conditions can also influence the timing of the harvest. It's best to harvest peaches during dry weather, as wet conditions can increase the risk of fruit rot and other post-harvest diseases. If rain is forecasted, it may be necessary to harvest the peaches a day or two earlier to avoid potential damage. Additionally, harvesting in the early morning or late afternoon, when temperatures are cooler, can help preserve the quality of the fruit and reduce the risk of bruising.

In commercial orchards, the harvest may be spread out over several weeks, with multiple pickings to ensure that each peach is harvested at its optimal stage of ripeness. This selective harvesting process ensures that only the best-quality fruit is picked, while allowing the remaining peaches to continue ripening on the tree. For home gardeners, harvesting can be done over a shorter period, but it's still important to pick the fruit in stages, rather than all at once, to ensure that each peach is at its best.

Harvesting Techniques

Harvesting peaches requires careful handling to ensure that the fruit remains unblemished and retains its high quality. Because peaches are delicate and bruise easily, it's important to use proper techniques when picking them from the tree. The first step in the harvesting process is to gently grasp the peach in the palm of the hand, taking care not to squeeze the fruit too firmly. Applying slight pressure with the fingertips, the peach should be twisted gently while being lifted upward. This twisting motion helps to separate the fruit from the branch without damaging the stem or the fruit itself.

If the peach does not easily detach from the branch with a gentle twist, it may not be fully ripe and could benefit from a few more days on the tree. It's important not to force the fruit off the branch, as this can cause bruising or damage to the stem, which can lead to premature spoilage. Using a soft, gloved hand can also help protect the fruit from bruising during the picking process. For higher branches, a fruit picker or a ladder may be necessary to reach the peaches without causing damage to the tree.

Once the peaches are picked, they should be handled with care to avoid bruising. It's best to place the peaches gently into a padded container, such as a basket lined with a soft cloth or foam, rather than dropping them into a hard container. Stacking the peaches too deeply in the container can cause the lower fruits to become bruised under the weight of the upper layers, so it's advisable to keep the layers shallow and to use multiple containers if needed. This careful handling is crucial for preserving the fruit's appearance and quality.

For commercial growers, the use of harvesting bags or bins with padded linings can help reduce the risk of bruising during the harvest. These containers are designed to be worn over the shoulder, allowing the picker to use both hands for harvesting while keeping the fruit secure and cushioned. The bags can be emptied gently into larger bins for transport to the packing area, where the peaches can be sorted and graded. This method helps streamline the harvesting process while ensuring that the fruit remains in optimal condition.

After harvesting, it's important to keep the peaches out of direct sunlight and heat, as high temperatures can cause the fruit to soften and deteriorate quickly. Peaches should be moved to a cool, shaded area as soon as possible after picking. In commercial operations, the fruit may be placed in refrigerated storage to extend its shelf life and maintain its quality until it can be processed or sold. For home gardeners, placing the peaches in a cool basement or refrigerator can help preserve their freshness for a longer period.

If the peaches are to be stored for any length of time, they should be inspected for any signs of damage or overripeness. Bruised or damaged fruit should be used immediately, as it will not store well and can lead to spoilage of other fruit in the storage container. Sorting the fruit based on ripeness and quality allows for better management of the harvest, with the ripest peaches being used first and the firmer fruit being stored for later use.

Using proper harvesting techniques is essential for ensuring that peaches retain their quality from the moment they are picked until they are consumed or sold. Gentle handling, careful storage, and attention to detail throughout the harvesting process help to maximize the flavor, texture, and shelf life of the fruit, resulting in a more successful and satisfying harvest.

Post-Harvest Care

After peaches are harvested, proper post-harvest care is essential to maintain their quality and extend their shelf life. One of the first steps in post-harvest care is to sort the fruit, removing any damaged, bruised, or overripe peaches. These fruits should be used immediately or processed into jams, preserves, or other products, as they will not store well. Sorting the peaches also helps prevent the spread of rot or spoilage to other fruits, ensuring that only the best-quality peaches are stored for later use or sale.

Cooling the peaches quickly after harvest is crucial for slowing down the ripening process and extending the fruit's shelf life. Peaches should be cooled to a temperature of around 32°F to 36°F as soon as possible after picking. This can be achieved by placing the peaches in a refrigerator or a cold storage area. Rapid cooling helps to preserve the fruit's firmness, flavor, and nutritional value, and reduces the risk of post-harvest diseases. For commercial growers, hydro-cooling or forced-air cooling methods may be used to achieve rapid cooling on a larger scale.

Humidity control is another important aspect of post-harvest care for peaches. Peaches have a high moisture content, and if stored in an environment that is too dry, they can lose moisture and become shriveled or leathery. On the other hand, if the humidity is too high, it can promote the growth of mold and other pathogens. The ideal relative humidity for storing peaches is around 90% to 95%. Maintaining this humidity level helps to keep the fruit plump and juicy while minimizing the risk of decay.

When storing peaches, it's important to keep them in a single layer or in shallow layers to avoid bruising and pressure damage. If the peaches are to be stored in multiple layers, placing soft pads or liners between the layers can help cushion the fruit and prevent damage. Storing peaches in ventilated containers, such as baskets or boxes with slats or holes, allows for better air circulation, which is important for preventing the buildup of ethylene gas—a natural plant hormone that accelerates ripening and can lead to premature spoilage.

Ethylene-sensitive fruits and vegetables, such as apples and bananas, should be stored separately from peaches, as they can produce ethylene gas that speeds up the ripening process. If peaches need to be ripened quickly for immediate use, placing them in a paper bag with an apple or banana can help concentrate the ethylene gas and hasten the ripening process. However, for extended storage, it's best to keep peaches away from ethylene-producing produce to ensure that they ripen slowly and evenly.

For peaches that will be sold or shipped, careful packaging is essential to protect the fruit during transport. Peaches should be packed in boxes or crates with dividers or padding to prevent them from moving around and becoming bruised. The boxes should be labeled with the harvest date and any relevant information about the variety or grade of the fruit. For long-distance shipping, refrigerated transport may be necessary to maintain the proper temperature and humidity levels throughout the journey.

Chapter 12

Health Benefits of Peaches

Nutritional Profile of Peaches

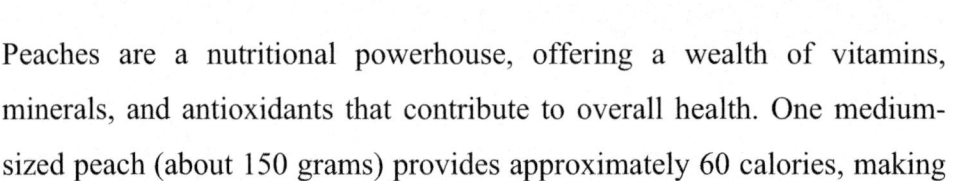

Health Benefits of Peaches

- Rich in fiber
- Low in calories
- Packed with vitamins
- High in potassium
- Contains antioxidants
- Boosts digestion
- Supports hydration
- Promotes heart health
- Improves skin health
- Strengthens immunity

Peaches are a nutritional powerhouse, offering a wealth of vitamins, minerals, and antioxidants that contribute to overall health. One medium-sized peach (about 150 grams) provides approximately 60 calories, making it a low-calorie option for those looking to maintain a healthy weight. Despite their low calorie content, peaches are rich in essential nutrients, including vitamin C, vitamin A, potassium, and dietary fiber. These nutrients play critical roles in various bodily functions, from boosting the immune system to supporting heart health.

Vitamin C is one of the most prominent nutrients found in peaches, with a single peach providing about 10% of the recommended daily intake. This vitamin is a potent antioxidant that helps protect cells from damage caused by free radicals. It also plays a vital role in collagen production, which is essential for maintaining healthy skin, blood vessels, and connective tissues. Regular consumption of vitamin C-rich foods like peaches can support the body's defense mechanisms and promote faster healing of wounds.

Peaches are also a good source of vitamin A, primarily in the form of beta-carotene, which the body converts into retinol, an active form of vitamin A. This vitamin is essential for maintaining healthy vision, particularly in low-light conditions. Beta-carotene also has antioxidant properties, helping to protect cells from oxidative stress and supporting the immune system. Including peaches in the diet can contribute to eye health and reduce the risk of age-related vision problems such as macular degeneration.

Potassium, another key nutrient in peaches, is crucial for maintaining proper fluid balance, nerve function, and muscle contractions. A medium-sized peach contains about 285 milligrams of potassium, which is approximately 6% of the daily recommended intake. Potassium is known for its role in regulating blood pressure by counteracting the effects of sodium. Consuming potassium-rich foods like peaches can help lower the risk of hypertension and support cardiovascular health.

Dietary fiber is another significant component of peaches, with each fruit providing around 2 grams of fiber. Fiber is essential for digestive health, as it aids in the movement of food through the digestive tract and helps prevent constipation. Soluble fiber, in particular, can help lower cholesterol levels by binding to cholesterol in the digestive system and preventing its absorption into the bloodstream. The fiber content in peaches also contributes to a feeling of fullness, making them a great addition to a weight management plan.

Peaches are also a source of lesser-known but equally important nutrients such as magnesium, phosphorus, and small amounts of iron. Magnesium is involved in over 300 enzymatic reactions in the body, including those that regulate muscle and nerve function, blood sugar levels, and blood pressure. Phosphorus is vital for the formation of bones and teeth, and it plays a role in energy production. Iron, although present in small amounts, is necessary for the production of hemoglobin, the protein in red blood cells that carries oxygen throughout the body.

The nutritional profile of peaches is further enhanced by their content of various antioxidants, including polyphenols and flavonoids. These compounds help reduce inflammation and protect against chronic diseases such as heart disease, diabetes, and certain types of cancer. The combination of vitamins, minerals, fiber, and antioxidants makes peaches a valuable addition to any diet, offering numerous health benefits while being naturally sweet and delicious.

Peaches and Digestive Health

Peaches are particularly beneficial for digestive health, thanks to their high fiber content and natural compounds that support the digestive system. The fiber in peaches is a mix of both soluble and insoluble fiber, each playing a unique role in maintaining digestive health. Insoluble fiber adds bulk to the stool, helping to prevent constipation by promoting regular bowel movements. This type of fiber passes through the digestive tract relatively intact, absorbing water and adding volume to the waste material, making it easier to pass.

Soluble fiber, on the other hand, dissolves in water to form a gel-like substance in the digestive tract. This gel slows down digestion, allowing for better absorption of nutrients and providing a steady release of energy. Soluble fiber also acts as a prebiotic, feeding the beneficial bacteria in the gut. A healthy balance of gut bacteria is essential for overall digestive health, as these microbes help break down food, produce vitamins, and protect against harmful pathogens. Regular consumption of peaches can contribute to a balanced gut microbiome, supporting digestive health and boosting immunity.

Peaches also contain natural sugars like sorbitol, which can have a mild laxative effect, helping to relieve constipation in some individuals. This makes peaches a gentle and natural option for those experiencing occasional digestive discomfort. Additionally, the water content in peaches—around 89%—helps keep the digestive tract hydrated, which is important for smooth digestion and preventing issues like constipation and bloating. Staying hydrated is key to maintaining a healthy digestive system, and the high water content in peaches makes them an excellent choice for promoting hydration.

The antioxidants in peaches, such as polyphenols and flavonoids, also play a role in supporting digestive health. These compounds help reduce inflammation in the gut, which can be beneficial for individuals with inflammatory bowel conditions like Crohn's disease or ulcerative colitis. By reducing inflammation, antioxidants can help protect the delicate lining of the digestive tract and promote healing of any existing damage. This anti-inflammatory effect also helps prevent the development of other digestive issues, such as gastritis and irritable bowel syndrome (IBS).

Peaches are also known for their ability to aid in digestion by promoting the secretion of digestive enzymes. These enzymes help break down food into smaller, more easily absorbed nutrients. For example, the enzyme amylase, found in peaches, assists in the digestion of carbohydrates, converting them into simple sugars that the body can use for energy. This enzymatic activity helps improve digestion efficiency and can reduce the likelihood of experiencing digestive discomfort after meals.

Another benefit of peaches for digestive health is their low acidity compared to other fruits. This makes them a suitable option for individuals with acid reflux or gastroesophageal reflux disease (GERD), who need to avoid highly acidic foods that can trigger symptoms. The gentle nature of peaches on the digestive system, combined with their natural sweetness, makes them an ideal fruit for those with sensitive stomachs or digestive issues.

Incorporating peaches into the diet can have a positive impact on digestive health, providing both immediate relief from minor digestive issues and long-term support for a healthy gut. The combination of fiber, water, antioxidants, and digestive enzymes in peaches makes them a valuable ally in maintaining a well-functioning digestive system.

Skin and Beauty Benefits

Peaches offer a range of skin and beauty benefits, making them a popular ingredient in both dietary regimens and skincare products. One of the primary reasons peaches are beneficial for the skin is their high vitamin C content. Vitamin C is essential for collagen production, a protein that gives the skin its structure and elasticity. As we age, collagen production naturally declines, leading to wrinkles and sagging skin. Including vitamin C-rich foods like peaches in the diet can help support collagen synthesis, keeping the skin firm, smooth, and youthful.

In addition to promoting collagen production, vitamin C also acts as a powerful antioxidant, protecting the skin from damage caused by free radicals. Free radicals are unstable molecules that can cause oxidative stress, leading to premature aging, hyperpigmentation, and a dull complexion. The antioxidants in peaches help neutralize these free radicals, reducing their harmful effects and promoting a more radiant and even skin tone. Regular consumption of peaches can contribute to a natural, healthy glow, making the skin appear more vibrant and rejuvenated.

Peaches are also a good source of vitamin A, which is vital for maintaining healthy skin. Vitamin A helps regulate the production of sebum, the natural oil produced by the skin, keeping it moisturized and preventing dryness. It also plays a role in cell turnover, encouraging the shedding of old skin cells and the growth of new ones. This process helps keep the skin smooth and clear, reducing the appearance of fine lines, acne, and other skin imperfections. For these reasons, vitamin A is often used in skincare products to treat conditions like acne and hyperpigmentation.

The natural sugars and acids in peaches also offer gentle exfoliating properties when applied topically. These compounds can help remove dead skin cells, unclog pores, and improve skin texture. Homemade peach masks or scrubs can be made by blending the fruit and applying it to the skin, allowing the natural enzymes and acids to work their magic. The result is softer, smoother skin with a more even tone. The mild nature of these natural exfoliants makes peaches suitable for all skin types, including sensitive skin.

Hydration is another key factor in maintaining healthy, youthful-looking skin, and the high water content in peaches makes them an excellent choice for keeping the skin hydrated from the inside out. Well-hydrated skin appears plumper and more radiant, with fewer visible fine lines and wrinkles. Drinking plenty of water and consuming water-rich fruits like peaches can help maintain the skin's moisture balance, preventing dryness and promoting a healthy complexion.

Peaches also contain a variety of other antioxidants, such as beta-carotene and polyphenols, which contribute to skin protection and repair. Beta-carotene, in particular, helps protect the skin from UV damage, reducing the risk of sunburn and long-term sun damage. While peaches should not replace sunscreen, consuming them regularly can provide an additional layer of protection against the harmful effects of the sun. This makes peaches a valuable addition to a skin-conscious diet, especially during the summer months when sun exposure is at its peak.

The combination of vitamins, antioxidants, and hydration provided by peaches makes them a powerful tool in promoting healthy, beautiful skin. Whether consumed as part of a balanced diet or applied topically in homemade skincare treatments, peaches offer a natural and effective way to enhance the skin's appearance and overall health.

Chapter 13

Delicious Ways to Enjoy Your Peaches

Fresh Peach Recipes

Fresh peaches are incredibly versatile and can be enjoyed in a variety of ways, whether eaten on their own or incorporated into delicious recipes. One of the simplest and most popular ways to enjoy fresh peaches is in a fruit salad. Combine sliced peaches with other seasonal fruits like berries, melons, and grapes for a refreshing and colorful dish that's perfect for breakfast or a light snack. To enhance the flavors, a drizzle of honey or a splash of lime juice can be added, along with fresh mint leaves for a burst of freshness.

Another classic way to enjoy fresh peaches is by grilling them. Grilling brings out the natural sweetness of the peaches and adds a subtle smoky flavor that pairs well with both sweet and savory dishes. To prepare, simply cut the peaches in half, remove the pit, and brush the cut sides with a little olive oil or melted butter. Place the peaches cut-side down on a hot grill and cook for a few minutes until they are slightly softened and have beautiful grill marks. Grilled peaches can be served as a side dish with grilled meats, added to salads, or topped with vanilla ice cream for a simple dessert.

Peach salsa is another delicious and unexpected way to use fresh peaches. Diced peaches can be combined with chopped tomatoes, red onion, jalapeños, cilantro, and lime juice for a sweet and tangy salsa that pairs perfectly with grilled chicken, fish, or tacos. The sweetness of the peaches balances the heat from the jalapeños, creating a flavorful and refreshing condiment that's perfect for summer. For an extra burst of flavor, try adding a touch of cumin or smoked paprika to the salsa.

Peach Salad and Peach Smoothie

For a refreshing summer drink, peaches can be used to make a fresh peach smoothie. Blend peeled and sliced peaches with yogurt, a splash of orange juice, and a handful of ice for a creamy, nutrient-packed smoothie that's perfect for breakfast or a post-workout snack. To add a little extra sweetness, a drizzle of honey or a few fresh berries can be included in the blend. The result is a delicious and healthy drink that's full of vitamins and antioxidants.

Peaches also make a delightful addition to salads, adding a sweet and juicy contrast to savory ingredients. One popular combination is a peach and arugula salad, where fresh peach slices are tossed with peppery arugula, crumbled feta cheese, toasted almonds, and a balsamic vinaigrette. The sweetness of the peaches complements the tangy feta and the slightly bitter arugula, creating a well-balanced salad that's both flavorful and satisfying. This salad is perfect as a light lunch or as a side dish for grilled meats.

For those with a sweet tooth, fresh peaches can be used to create a simple yet elegant dessert of peach parfaits. Layer sliced peaches with Greek yogurt, granola, and a drizzle of honey in individual glasses for a healthy and delicious treat. The creaminess of the yogurt, the crunch of the granola, and the sweetness of the peaches create a delightful combination of textures and flavors. These parfaits are easy to prepare and can be made ahead of time, making them a great option for entertaining or a quick dessert.

Fresh peaches offer endless possibilities in the kitchen, from simple snacks to creative dishes that highlight their natural sweetness and flavor. Whether enjoyed raw, grilled, or blended, peaches add a burst of summer freshness to any meal.

Baking with Peaches

Baking with peaches brings out their natural sweetness and juiciness, making them a perfect ingredient for a variety of desserts and baked goods. One of the most beloved peach desserts is the classic peach cobbler. This comforting dish features a layer of sweet, tender peaches topped with a buttery, biscuit-like crust. To make a peach cobbler, start by tossing sliced peaches with sugar, a touch of cinnamon, and a squeeze of lemon juice. The peaches are then placed in a baking dish and topped with dollops of biscuit dough or a crumbly streusel topping. As the cobbler bakes, the peaches release their juices, creating a luscious filling that pairs perfectly with the golden, flaky crust.

Peach pie is a classic dessert made with fresh, juicy peaches.

Peach pie is another timeless dessert that showcases the fruit's natural flavor. A well-made peach pie features a flaky, buttery crust filled with a generous amount of sweet, juicy peaches. To prepare, slice fresh peaches and toss them with sugar, a bit of flour or cornstarch to thicken the filling, and a dash of cinnamon or nutmeg for added warmth. The peach filling is then placed in a pie crust and topped with either a lattice crust or a full top crust. Baking the pie until the crust is golden and the filling is bubbling creates a dessert that's perfect for summer gatherings and family dinners.

For a lighter, more delicate dessert, peach tartlets offer an elegant presentation and a burst of fresh flavor. These individual-sized tarts are made by filling mini tart shells with a mixture of fresh peaches, sugar, and a hint of vanilla. The tartlets are baked until the crust is golden and the peaches are tender and caramelized. For an extra touch of indulgence, the tartlets can be finished with a dollop of whipped cream or a scoop of vanilla ice cream. These petite desserts are perfect for serving at parties or as a special treat after dinner.

Peach muffins are a wonderful way to incorporate peaches into breakfast or brunch. These moist, tender muffins are made by folding diced peaches into a simple muffin batter, which can be enhanced with spices like cinnamon, ginger, or nutmeg. The muffins can be topped with a sprinkle of coarse sugar or a crumbly streusel for added texture and sweetness. Baking the muffins until golden and fragrant results in a delicious, fruit-filled treat that's perfect for enjoying with a cup of coffee or tea.

Another delightful option for baking with peaches is a peach upside-down cake. This visually stunning cake features slices of fresh peaches arranged in a decorative pattern on the bottom of the cake pan, which is then topped with a rich, buttery cake batter. As the cake bakes, the peaches caramelize, creating a beautiful, golden topping that's revealed when the cake is inverted onto a serving plate. The combination of the tender cake and the sweet, caramelized peaches makes this dessert a showstopper at any gathering.

Peach scones are another delicious way to enjoy baked peaches. These tender, flaky scones are made by incorporating diced peaches into a simple scone dough, along with a touch of cream and a hint of vanilla or almond extract. The scones are baked until golden and slightly crisp on the outside, with a soft, peach-studded interior. Serving the scones warm with a drizzle of honey or a dollop of clotted cream makes for a delightful breakfast or afternoon snack.

Baking with peaches allows their natural sweetness and flavor to shine, creating desserts and baked goods that are both comforting and delicious. Whether in a cobbler, pie, tartlet, or muffin, peaches add a touch of summer to any baked treat, making them a favorite ingredient for bakers and dessert lovers alike.

Preserving Your Peaches

Preserving peaches is a wonderful way to enjoy their sweet, juicy flavor long after the harvest season has ended. One of the most popular methods of preservation is canning. Canned peaches can be enjoyed on their own, used in desserts, or added to recipes throughout the year. To can peaches, start by peeling and slicing the fruit, then packing the slices into sterilized jars. A light syrup made of sugar and water is poured over the peaches to preserve their texture and flavor. The jars are then processed in a water bath canner to seal them and ensure their safety for long-term storage. Canned peaches can last for up to a year when stored in a cool, dark place, making them a convenient option for enjoying summer's bounty all year round.

Freezing peaches is another easy and effective method of preservation. Frozen peaches retain much of their fresh flavor and can be used in smoothies, baked goods, or as a topping for yogurt and oatmeal. To freeze peaches, start by peeling and slicing the fruit. Lay the slices in a single layer on a baking sheet and freeze them until firm. Once frozen, the peach slices can be transferred to freezer bags or containers for long-term storage. Adding a bit of lemon juice to the peaches before freezing can help prevent browning. Frozen peaches can be kept in the freezer for up to a year, providing a taste of summer even in the depths of winter.

Making peach jam or preserves is another delicious way to capture the essence of fresh peaches. Peach jam is made by cooking peeled and chopped peaches with sugar and lemon juice until the mixture thickens to a spreadable consistency. Pectin may be added to help the jam set, though some recipes rely on the natural pectin in the fruit. Once the jam reaches the desired consistency, it's poured into sterilized jars and processed in a water bath canner to ensure a proper seal. The result is a sweet, tangy spread that's perfect for toast, scones, or as a filling for pastries.

Dehydrating peaches is a method of preservation that results in chewy, flavorful peach slices that can be enjoyed as a snack or added to trail mix, granola, or baked goods. To dehydrate peaches, start by peeling and slicing the fruit into uniform pieces. The slices are then placed on dehydrator trays and dried at a low temperature until they are leathery but still pliable.

Dehydrated peaches should be stored in an airtight container in a cool, dark place, where they can last for several months. The concentrated flavor of dehydrated peaches makes them a satisfying and healthy snack.

Another way to preserve peaches is by making peach butter. Similar to apple butter, peach butter is a thick, smooth spread made by cooking peaches slowly with sugar and spices until the mixture reduces and thickens. The result is a rich, intensely flavored spread that's perfect for spreading on toast, pancakes, or biscuits. Peach butter can be canned for long-term storage or kept in the refrigerator for immediate use. The deep, concentrated flavor of peach butter makes it a special treat that captures the essence of ripe, summer peaches.

For those who enjoy a bit of fermentation, peach wine or peach liqueur can be made by fermenting fresh peaches with sugar and yeast. The process of fermentation transforms the sugars in the peaches into alcohol, resulting in a fruity, aromatic beverage that can be enjoyed on its own or used in cocktails. Peach wine can be bottled and aged for several months to develop its flavor, while peach liqueur can be enjoyed sooner after a shorter fermentation period. Both options offer a unique and delicious way to preserve the flavor of peaches in a form that can be savored year-round.

Preserving peaches through canning, freezing, dehydrating, or fermenting allows their sweet, summery flavor to be enjoyed long after the fresh fruit is gone. Each method of preservation offers its own unique way to savor peaches, making them a versatile and cherished fruit in kitchens everywhere.

Chapter 14

Year-Round Peach Tree Care

Seasonal Care Calendar

Caring for peach trees is a year-round commitment that requires attention to seasonal changes and specific tasks that ensure the tree's health and productivity. A well-planned seasonal care calendar helps gardeners stay on top of these tasks, making it easier to manage the tree's needs throughout the year. Each season brings its own set of responsibilities, from pruning and fertilizing to monitoring for pests and diseases. By breaking down peach tree care into seasonal tasks, growers can provide the right care at the right time, ensuring a bountiful harvest.

In winter, the focus is on preparing the tree for dormancy and protecting it from cold weather. This is the time for pruning, which should be done during the tree's dormant period, typically in late winter. Pruning helps to shape the tree, remove dead or diseased wood, and encourage new growth in the spring. It's also the season to apply dormant oil sprays to control overwintering pests and diseases. Protecting the tree's roots and trunk from freezing temperatures with mulch and trunk wraps is also crucial in areas prone to severe cold.

As spring arrives, the tree begins to wake from dormancy, and this is when gardeners need to focus on promoting healthy growth. Fertilizing the tree with a balanced fertilizer is essential to give it the nutrients it needs for vigorous growth and fruit production. Spring is also the time to monitor for

106

early signs of pests and diseases and apply preventive treatments if necessary. As the tree blooms, thinning fruit and adjusting irrigation are important tasks to ensure that the tree produces high-quality fruit.

Summer is a critical time for peach tree care, as the tree is actively growing and producing fruit. During this season, the focus shifts to regular watering, especially during dry spells, and maintaining proper soil moisture levels. Mulching helps to conserve moisture and keep the soil cool. It's also important to continue monitoring for pests and diseases, as summer is when many of these problems can become more pronounced. In some cases, additional fertilization may be necessary to support the tree's fruit production.

Autumn is a time of transition as the tree prepares to enter dormancy once again. After the harvest, it's important to clean up fallen leaves and fruit to reduce the risk of pests and diseases overwintering in the debris. This is also the time to conduct a final inspection for any remaining pests or diseases and apply treatments if needed. Fertilizing the tree with a low-nitrogen fertilizer can help to strengthen the tree's roots and prepare it for winter. In late autumn, it's important to begin winterizing tasks, such as applying mulch and trunk wraps, to protect the tree from cold damage.

Following a seasonal care calendar helps ensure that peach trees receive the right care at the right time. This structured approach not only simplifies the management of peach trees but also promotes their long-term health and productivity, leading to better fruit yields year after year.

Winterizing Your Peach Trees

Winter can be a challenging season for peach trees, especially in regions with harsh cold or fluctuating temperatures. Winterizing your peach trees is essential to protect them from freezing temperatures, frost damage, and potential winter injury. One of the first steps in winterizing is applying a thick layer of mulch around the base of the tree. Mulch acts as an insulator, protecting the roots from extreme cold and helping to regulate soil temperature. Organic mulches like straw, wood chips, or pine needles are ideal for this purpose, and they should be applied in a layer about 3 to 4 inches thick.

Trunk protection is another critical aspect of winterizing peach trees. Young trees, in particular, are susceptible to sunscald and frost cracks, which occur when the sun warms the trunk during the day and the temperature drops rapidly at night. To prevent this, the trunk should be wrapped with a tree wrap or burlap, starting from the base and extending up to the first branches. This protective barrier helps to reflect sunlight and insulate the trunk, reducing the risk of damage. The wrap should be removed in early spring once the risk of frost has passed.

In addition to physical protection, it's important to ensure that the tree is well-hydrated before the onset of winter. A deep watering in late autumn, before the ground freezes, can help to prevent winter desiccation, which occurs when the tree loses moisture through its branches and leaves but cannot replace it from the frozen soil. Proper hydration helps the tree withstand cold temperatures and reduces the risk of winter injury.

However, avoid overwatering, as this can lead to root rot if the soil becomes waterlogged.

Pruning during the winter is another important task, but it should be done carefully to avoid stimulating new growth that could be damaged by frost. Late winter, when the tree is fully dormant but before the buds start to swell, is the best time for pruning. Focus on removing dead, diseased, or damaged wood, as well as any branches that could cause problems during the growing season. This pruning not only helps to shape the tree but also reduces the risk of disease by improving air circulation and light penetration in the canopy.

For trees in particularly cold regions, additional protection may be necessary. One option is to create a windbreak using burlap or other materials to shield the tree from harsh winds, which can exacerbate the effects of cold temperatures. Another strategy is to use anti-desiccant sprays, which create a protective barrier on the leaves and branches to reduce moisture loss. These sprays are especially useful for evergreen peach varieties or in regions where winter winds are a significant concern.

Monitoring the weather is an important part of winterizing peach trees. Being aware of sudden temperature drops or unseasonal warm spells can help you take timely action to protect your trees. If a severe cold snap is predicted, additional insulation, such as covering the tree with blankets or horticultural fleece, may be necessary. Conversely, if there is an unexpected warm spell, it's important to avoid removing any protective coverings too early, as this could expose the tree to subsequent cold damage.

Springtime Boosts

Spring is a time of renewal and growth for peach trees, and providing the right care during this season is crucial for setting the stage for a successful harvest. One of the first tasks in spring is to remove any winter protective coverings, such as mulch or trunk wraps, once the danger of frost has passed. This allows the soil to warm up and the tree to begin its growth cycle without the risk of overheating. It's also a good time to check the tree for any signs of winter damage, such as frost cracks or dieback, and to address these issues promptly.

Fertilizing in the spring is essential to give the peach tree the nutrients it needs to support new growth and fruit development. A balanced fertilizer with a higher nitrogen content is typically recommended, as nitrogen promotes vigorous leaf and shoot growth. Applying the fertilizer just as the buds begin to swell ensures that the tree has access to the nutrients it needs during the critical early stages of growth. For best results, the fertilizer should be spread evenly around the tree's drip line and lightly worked into the soil, followed by thorough watering.

As the tree begins to bloom, it's important to monitor for pests and diseases, which can quickly take hold during the warm, wet conditions of spring. Common springtime pests include aphids, peach twig borers, and oriental fruit moths, all of which can cause significant damage if not controlled early. Using organic or chemical treatments, such as insecticidal soaps or horticultural oils, can help to manage these pests. Additionally, applying fungicides during the bloom period can help prevent common diseases like peach leaf curl and brown rot, which thrive in the damp conditions of spring.

Thinning the fruit is another important task during the spring. Once the tree has set fruit, it's important to thin out excess peaches to ensure that the remaining fruit can grow to full size and quality. Ideally, peaches should be spaced about 6 to 8 inches apart on the branches. Thinning also helps to prevent branch breakage by reducing the weight of the fruit on the tree. This task should be done carefully, using clean, sharp tools to avoid damaging the branches or fruit.

Irrigation becomes increasingly important as the weather warms and the tree's growth accelerates. While peach trees require less water during the early spring, as the leaves and fruit develop, their water needs increase. It's important to keep the soil consistently moist but not waterlogged, as overly wet conditions can lead to root rot. Using drip irrigation or soaker hoses can help deliver water directly to the root zone, minimizing water waste and reducing the risk of disease.

Pruning in the spring is generally limited to removing any damaged or diseased wood that wasn't addressed during the winter. However, light pruning to improve air circulation and sunlight penetration may be beneficial, especially if the tree's canopy is dense. This can help reduce the risk of fungal diseases and promote more even ripening of the fruit. Spring pruning should be done with care to avoid removing too much growth, as this can reduce the tree's ability to produce fruit.

Providing these springtime boosts sets the foundation for a healthy, productive peach tree that will thrive throughout the growing season. With proper fertilization, pest and disease management, thinning, and irrigation, the tree will be well-equipped to produce a bountiful harvest of delicious peaches.

Chapter 15

Propagating Peach Trees

Grafting Basics

Grafting is one of the most widely used methods for peach propagation.

Grafting is a widely used method for propagating peach trees, allowing gardeners to create new trees with specific desirable traits, such as improved fruit quality, disease resistance, or adaptability to certain climates. The basic principle of grafting involves joining the tissue of one plant, known as the scion, to the rootstock of another plant. The scion, typically a branch or bud from a peach tree with desirable characteristics, is carefully attached to the rootstock, which provides the root system for the new tree. Over time, the two parts grow together, forming a single, unified plant.

One of the most common grafting techniques used for peach trees is the whip and tongue graft, which is typically performed in late winter or early spring when the tree is still dormant. To perform this graft, both the scion and the rootstock are cut at a diagonal angle, creating a long, smooth surface. A small tongue-like notch is then cut into both the scion and the rootstock, allowing them to interlock when joined. This technique creates a strong union between the two parts, increasing the chances of successful grafting. The graft is then secured with grafting tape or rubber bands, and the exposed area is sealed with grafting wax to prevent moisture loss and infection.

Another popular grafting method for peach trees is the bud graft, also known as T-budding. This method is often performed in late summer, when the tree is actively growing. In T-budding, a single bud from the scion is inserted into a T-shaped incision made in the bark of the rootstock. The bud is then secured with grafting tape, leaving it exposed to grow and eventually form a new shoot. T-budding is a relatively simple and efficient method, making it a favorite among gardeners who are new to grafting.

Grafting offers several advantages over other methods of propagation. One of the key benefits is that it allows for the propagation of peach trees with specific, desirable traits, such as improved fruit flavor, disease resistance, or cold hardiness. Additionally, grafting can speed up the time it takes for a peach tree to bear fruit, as the scion comes from a mature tree that is already capable of fruiting. This makes grafting an ideal method for gardeners looking to establish a productive orchard more quickly.

However, grafting also requires careful attention to detail and proper technique to be successful. It's important to select healthy, disease-free scion and rootstock material, as any diseases present in the parent plants can be transmitted to the new tree. The grafting cuts must be made with clean, sharp tools to ensure a smooth, even surface that will heal properly. Aftercare is also crucial, as the graft must be protected from pests, diseases, and environmental stress while it heals and begins to grow.

Despite its challenges, grafting is a highly rewarding method of propagating peach trees, offering gardeners the opportunity to create customized trees that meet their specific needs. With practice and patience, even novice gardeners can learn to graft successfully, adding new and unique peach varieties to their orchards.

Growing from Seed

Growing peach trees from seed is a more time-consuming and uncertain method of propagation, but it can be a rewarding way to explore new varieties or simply enjoy the process of nurturing a tree from the very beginning. Unlike grafting, which produces a clone of the parent tree, growing from seed introduces genetic variation, meaning the resulting tree may not produce fruit identical to that of the parent. However, this method offers the potential for discovering new and unique peach varieties, as well as the satisfaction of growing a tree entirely from scratch.

The first step in growing a peach tree from seed is to obtain a healthy, ripe peach. The pit inside the fruit contains the seed, which can be carefully extracted by cracking open the pit with a hammer or nutcracker. It's important to avoid damaging the seed inside, as a damaged seed is unlikely to germinate. Once the seed is extracted, it should be cleaned of any remaining fruit pulp and allowed to dry for a few days before planting.

Peach seeds require a period of cold stratification to break dormancy and encourage germination. This mimics the natural winter conditions the seed would experience if left outdoors. To stratify the seed, it should be placed in a plastic bag with a moist medium, such as sand or peat moss, and stored in the refrigerator for several weeks to three months. The temperature should be kept between 34°F and 40°F to ensure successful stratification. During this time, the seed should be checked periodically to ensure it remains moist but not waterlogged.

Once the cold stratification period is complete, the seed can be planted in a pot or directly in the ground, depending on the climate and growing conditions. If planting in a pot, a well-draining potting mix is essential to prevent root rot. The seed should be planted about 1 to 2 inches deep, with the pointed end facing downward. Regular watering is important to keep the soil consistently moist, but not soggy. It may take several weeks to a few months for the seed to germinate, so patience is key.

As the seedling grows, it will require proper care to ensure its health and development. This includes regular watering, adequate sunlight, and protection from pests and diseases. Once the seedling has grown large enough, it can be transplanted into the ground or a larger pot, where it will continue to grow and develop. It's important to provide the young tree with support, such as a stake, to help it grow straight and strong.

One of the challenges of growing peach trees from seed is the unpredictability of the fruit. Because the seed is the result of cross-pollination, the fruit it produces may differ significantly from that of the parent tree. This means that the fruit's size, flavor, and quality can vary, and it may take several years for the tree to produce fruit. However, this variability also offers the potential for discovering new and unique peach varieties that may have desirable traits.

Growing peach trees from seed is a process that requires patience and care, but it can be a deeply rewarding experience. Whether for the challenge, the potential discovery of a new variety, or simply the joy of nurturing a tree from seed to maturity, this method of propagation offers a unique opportunity for gardeners to connect with nature and enjoy the fruits of their labor.

Propagating by Cuttings

Propagating peach trees by cuttings is a method that offers a balance between the speed of grafting and the simplicity of growing from seed. This technique involves taking a cutting from a healthy peach tree and encouraging it to develop roots, eventually growing into a new tree that is genetically identical to the parent. Propagating by cuttings is a straightforward process that can be done with minimal equipment, making it an accessible option for both novice and experienced gardeners.

The first step in propagating by cuttings is to select a healthy branch from the parent tree. The best time to take cuttings is in late spring or early summer, when the tree is actively growing. The cutting should be about 6 to 8 inches long and taken from a branch that is relatively new but has begun to harden off—this means it's neither too soft nor too woody. Using a sharp, clean pair of pruning shears, the cutting should be taken just below a node, which is the point where a leaf or bud is attached to the branch.

Once the cutting is taken, the lower leaves should be removed, leaving only a few leaves at the top to reduce moisture loss. The cut end of the cutting can then be dipped in rooting hormone, which encourages root development and increases the chances of successful propagation. While rooting hormone is not strictly necessary, it can significantly improve the success rate, especially for more challenging species like peach trees.

The cutting is then planted in a pot filled with a well-draining potting mix, such as a mix of peat moss and perlite. The cutting should be inserted into the soil so that at least one node is buried, as this is where the roots will form. The soil should be kept consistently moist but not waterlogged, and the pot should be placed in a warm, bright location out of direct sunlight. To create a humid environment that encourages rooting, the pot can be covered with a plastic bag or placed in a propagator.

Root development typically takes several weeks to a few months, depending on the conditions and the cutting itself. During this time, it's important to monitor the cutting for signs of new growth, which indicates that roots are forming. Once the cutting has developed a healthy root system and begins to produce new leaves, it can be gradually acclimated to outdoor conditions before being transplanted into the ground or a larger pot.

Propagating peach trees by cuttings offers several advantages, including the ability to replicate the exact characteristics of the parent tree. This is particularly valuable for preserving desirable traits such as fruit quality, disease resistance, or specific growth habits. Unlike growing from seed, which introduces genetic variation, propagating by cuttings ensures that the new tree will produce fruit identical to that of the parent.

However, this method also comes with challenges, such as the need for precise care during the rooting process and the potential for lower success rates compared to other propagation methods. Not all cuttings will successfully root, and some may require multiple attempts to achieve the desired results. Providing the right conditions, such as humidity, warmth, and adequate light, is crucial to improving the chances of success.

Propagating peach trees by cuttings is a rewarding technique that allows gardeners to expand their orchards with clones of their favorite trees. With careful attention to detail and proper care, this method can produce strong, healthy trees that will bear fruit for years to come.

Chapter 16

Growing Peaches in Containers

Choosing the Right Container

Growing a Peach Tree in a Container

Growing peach trees in containers offers a flexible and rewarding way to cultivate these delicious fruits, especially for those with limited space or who wish to move their trees to protect them from harsh weather. The first and most crucial step in successful container gardening is selecting the right container for your peach tree. The container you choose will directly impact the tree's growth, health, and fruit production, so it's important to make an informed decision.

The size of the container is one of the most critical factors to consider. A peach tree requires ample space for its root system to expand, so the container should be large enough to accommodate this growth. For a young peach tree, a container with a minimum diameter of 18 to 24 inches and a similar depth is recommended. As the tree matures, it may need to be repotted into a larger container, ideally 24 to 30 inches in diameter, to ensure it has enough room to thrive. Larger containers also help stabilize the tree, reducing the risk of tipping over in windy conditions.

Material is another important consideration when choosing a container. Containers are available in a variety of materials, including plastic, terracotta, wood, and ceramic. Each material has its pros and cons. Plastic containers are lightweight, durable, and retain moisture well, but they can heat up quickly in direct sunlight, potentially harming the roots. Terracotta pots are porous, allowing for better air circulation around the roots, but they tend to dry out faster and are heavier to move. Wooden containers offer good insulation against temperature fluctuations and a natural aesthetic, but they may require more maintenance to prevent rot. Ceramic containers are attractive and stable but can be heavy and prone to cracking in freezing temperatures.

Drainage is a crucial aspect of container gardening. Peach trees require well-draining soil to prevent root rot and other water-related issues. Therefore, the container must have adequate drainage holes at the bottom to allow excess water to escape. If the container lacks sufficient drainage, it can lead to waterlogged soil, which is detrimental to the tree's health. To enhance drainage, consider placing a layer of gravel or broken pottery shards at the bottom of the container before adding soil.

The weight of the container, especially when filled with soil and a mature tree, is another practical consideration. While heavier containers provide stability, they can be challenging to move. To make relocation easier, particularly for those who may need to move the container indoors during winter, consider using a container with wheels or placing it on a plant dolly. This will allow you to move the tree without straining your back or damaging the container.

Choosing a container with a light color can help reflect sunlight and prevent the roots from overheating, which is particularly important in hot climates. Dark-colored containers absorb heat, which can raise the soil temperature and stress the tree, especially during the summer months. If a dark container is the only option, consider placing it in a shaded area during the hottest part of the day or wrapping it in a reflective material.

The aesthetics of the container should not be overlooked, as it will likely become a prominent feature in your garden or patio. While functionality is key, choosing a container that complements your outdoor space can enhance the overall look of your garden. Consider the style, color, and texture of the container, and how it will fit with the surrounding environment.

Container Care Tips

Caring for peach trees in containers requires attention to detail and consistent maintenance, as the confined space of a container presents unique challenges that differ from in-ground planting. One of the primary concerns is ensuring that the tree receives adequate water. Container-grown peach trees tend to dry out more quickly than those planted in the ground, especially during hot weather. Therefore, regular watering is essential. The frequency of watering depends on the size of the container, the tree's growth stage, and the weather conditions. Typically, the soil should be kept consistently moist but not waterlogged. A good rule of thumb is to water the tree when the top inch of soil feels dry to the touch.

To help retain moisture and reduce the frequency of watering, mulching is highly beneficial. A layer of organic mulch, such as wood chips, straw, or compost, placed on the surface of the soil helps to conserve moisture, regulate soil temperature, and suppress weed growth. Be sure to keep the mulch a few inches away from the trunk to prevent rot and pest issues. Mulching also improves the overall health of the soil by gradually breaking down and adding nutrients.

Fertilization is another critical aspect of container care. Peach trees in containers rely on the nutrients provided through fertilization since they cannot access nutrients from the surrounding soil as in-ground trees do. A balanced, slow-release fertilizer designed for fruit trees should be applied during the growing season to support healthy growth and fruit production. Typically, fertilization should begin in early spring as new growth starts and continue through the summer. Be cautious not to over-fertilize, as this can lead to excessive leaf growth at the expense of fruit production and can potentially burn the roots.

Pruning is essential for maintaining the size and shape of container-grown peach trees. Regular pruning helps to keep the tree compact, encourages the growth of fruiting wood, and improves air circulation, which reduces the risk of disease. Pruning should be done in late winter or early spring before the tree breaks dormancy. Focus on removing dead, damaged, or diseased branches, as well as thinning out crowded areas to allow light and air to penetrate the canopy. For container-grown trees, it's also important to prune the roots periodically. Every two to three years, consider repotting the tree and trimming back the roots to prevent it from becoming root-bound.

Another important care tip is to monitor for pests and diseases, which can be more prevalent in the confined environment of a container. Common pests that affect peach trees include aphids, spider mites, and peach tree borers. Regularly inspect the tree, especially the undersides of leaves and around the base, for signs of pest activity. Using organic pest control methods, such as insecticidal soaps or neem oil, can help manage infestations without harming beneficial insects. Additionally, maintaining proper hygiene, such as removing fallen leaves and fruit, can reduce the risk of diseases like peach leaf curl and brown rot.

Container-grown peach trees may require additional protection during the winter months, especially in regions with freezing temperatures. Since the roots are more exposed to the cold in a container, it's important to insulate the container or move it to a sheltered location, such as a garage or greenhouse. Wrapping the container with insulating materials like burlap or bubble wrap can help protect the roots from freezing. Alternatively, if the container is too large to move, placing it against a south-facing wall or in a sheltered corner of the garden can provide some protection from the cold.

Best Varieties for Containers

Not all peach tree varieties are suitable for container growing, as some can grow too large or require more extensive root systems than a container can accommodate. When choosing a variety for container gardening, it's important to select dwarf or semi-dwarf varieties that are naturally smaller and more manageable. These varieties are specifically bred for compact growth, making them ideal for containers and small spaces.

One of the best varieties for container growing is the 'Bonanza' dwarf peach tree. This variety is known for its compact size, reaching only about 4 to 6 feet in height at maturity, making it perfect for container gardening. Despite its small stature, 'Bonanza' produces full-sized, sweet, and juicy peaches that are excellent for fresh eating or cooking. The tree is also highly ornamental, with showy pink blossoms in the spring, making it a beautiful addition to any patio or balcony.

The 'Pixzee' dwarf peach tree is another excellent choice for container growing. Like 'Bonanza,' 'Pixzee' is a naturally compact tree, growing to about 4 to 5 feet in height. It produces large, flavorful peaches with a yellow flesh that is perfect for fresh eating, baking, or canning. The tree is self-fertile, meaning it does not require another peach tree for pollination, making it a convenient option for those with limited space. 'Pixzee' is also relatively hardy, with good disease resistance, making it a low-maintenance choice for container gardening.

'Honey Babe' is another popular dwarf peach variety that is well-suited for container growing. This variety is known for its sweet, honey-flavored peaches and its compact size, typically growing to about 5 to 6 feet tall. 'Honey Babe' is a prolific producer, yielding a good crop of medium-sized peaches each year. It is also a self-fertile variety, so only one tree is needed to produce fruit. The tree's attractive foliage and blossoms make it a lovely ornamental plant, as well as a productive fruit tree.

For those looking for a slightly larger tree, the semi-dwarf 'Empress' peach is an excellent choice. This variety can grow to about 8 to 10 feet in height but can be kept smaller with regular pruning, making it suitable for larger containers. 'Empress' is known for its large, juicy peaches with a rich, sweet flavor. The tree is also highly productive and disease-resistant, making it a reliable choice for container gardening. Its slightly larger size makes it a good option for those who want a more substantial tree in their container garden.

The 'Garden Gold' peach is another variety that works well in containers. This semi-dwarf tree typically grows to about 6 to 8 feet tall and produces abundant crops of golden-yellow peaches with a sweet, tangy flavor. 'Garden Gold' is self-fertile and relatively easy to grow, making it a good choice for beginners. The tree's attractive golden fruit and compact size make it a standout in any container garden.

Selecting the right variety is key to successful container gardening with peach trees. Dwarf and semi-dwarf varieties like 'Bonanza,' 'Pixzee,' 'Honey Babe,' 'Empress,' and 'Garden Gold' offer the perfect combination of manageable size, high yield, and delicious fruit. By choosing a variety that fits well within the constraints of a container, gardeners can enjoy the rewards of fresh, homegrown peaches even in limited spaces.

Chapter 17

Peach Trees and Companion Planting

Best Companion Plants for Peaches

Growing a Peach Tree With Companion Plants

Companion planting is a time-tested gardening technique that involves growing certain plants together to enhance growth, repel pests, and improve the overall health of the garden. Peach trees, like many other fruit trees, can benefit from the presence of specific companion plants that help create a more balanced and productive growing environment. Choosing the right companions for your peach tree can lead to healthier trees, better fruit yields, and a more diverse and resilient garden ecosystem.

One of the best companion plants for peach trees is the marigold (*Tagetes spp.*). Marigolds are well-known for their pest-repellent properties, particularly against nematodes, which can damage the roots of peach trees. The roots of marigolds release a natural compound that deters nematodes, helping to protect the peach tree from root damage. Additionally, marigolds attract beneficial insects such as ladybugs and parasitic wasps, which prey on aphids, caterpillars, and other common peach tree pests. Their bright, cheerful flowers also add visual appeal to the garden, making marigolds a valuable companion for peach trees.

Another excellent companion for peach trees is garlic (*Allium sativum*). Garlic is a powerful natural pest repellent, known for deterring a wide range of insects, including aphids, mites, and Japanese beetles, which can damage peach trees. The strong scent of garlic confuses pests and makes the area around the peach tree less attractive to them. Planting garlic at the base of peach trees or interspersed throughout the orchard can create a protective barrier that helps keep harmful insects at bay. Additionally, garlic has antifungal properties that can help reduce the incidence of fungal diseases like peach leaf curl.

Comfrey (*Symphytum officinale*) is another beneficial companion plant for peach trees. Comfrey is a deep-rooted perennial that mines nutrients from deep within the soil, bringing them up to the surface where they can be used by neighboring plants. When comfrey leaves are cut back and used as mulch around peach trees, they release these nutrients, particularly potassium, which is essential for fruit development. Comfrey also helps improve soil structure and moisture retention, creating a healthier growing environment for peach trees. Its flowers attract pollinators and beneficial insects, adding to its value as a companion plant.

Nasturtiums (*Tropaeolum majus*) are a great companion plant for peach trees, particularly in pest management. Nasturtiums are known for attracting aphids away from fruit trees, acting as a trap crop that protects the peach tree from aphid infestations. The presence of nasturtiums can also help deter other pests, such as whiteflies and squash bugs. Additionally, nasturtiums are edible and can be used in salads, making them a multifunctional addition to the garden. Their vibrant flowers also attract pollinators, which are essential for peach tree pollination and fruit set.

Chives (*Allium schoenoprasum*) are another effective companion plant for peach trees. Like garlic, chives have strong pest-repelling properties, particularly against aphids and other sap-sucking insects. The sulfur compounds in chives help to deter these pests and reduce the risk of fungal infections. Chives are also a low-maintenance perennial that can be planted around the base of peach trees, creating an attractive and functional ground cover. The flowers of chives attract bees and other pollinators, further enhancing the productivity of the peach tree.

By choosing the right companion plants for your peach tree, you can create a more harmonious and productive garden. Marigolds, garlic, comfrey, nasturtiums, and chives are all excellent choices that offer a range of benefits, from pest control to nutrient enhancement. These plants not only support the health and growth of the peach tree but also contribute to a more diverse and resilient garden ecosystem.

Companion Planting Benefits

Companion planting offers a variety of benefits that can enhance the health, productivity, and resilience of peach trees and the surrounding garden ecosystem. One of the most significant advantages of companion planting is natural pest control. By strategically planting pest-repelling herbs, flowers, and vegetables near peach trees, gardeners can reduce the need for chemical pesticides. Plants like garlic, marigolds, and nasturtiums release natural compounds that deter pests, while also attracting beneficial insects that prey on common peach tree pests. This integrated approach to pest management helps protect the peach tree from damage while promoting a more balanced and sustainable garden environment.

Another key benefit of companion planting is improved pollination. Peach trees rely on pollinators, such as bees and butterflies, to transfer pollen from one flower to another, leading to successful fruit set. Companion plants like chives, comfrey, and marigolds attract these important pollinators, ensuring that peach flowers receive the necessary attention during the blooming period. By enhancing pollinator activity in the garden, companion planting can lead to increased fruit yields and better-quality peaches.

Soil health is another area where companion planting shines. Certain companion plants, like comfrey and legumes, help improve soil fertility by adding nutrients to the soil. Comfrey, for example, is rich in potassium, an essential nutrient for fruit development. When comfrey leaves are used as mulch, they release these nutrients into the soil, benefiting the peach tree.

Legumes, such as beans and peas, have the ability to fix nitrogen in the soil, enriching it with this vital nutrient and reducing the need for synthetic fertilizers. Healthier soil leads to stronger, more resilient peach trees that are better equipped to withstand pests, diseases, and environmental stressors.

Companion planting also enhances biodiversity in the garden, which is crucial for maintaining a healthy ecosystem. A diverse garden is more resilient to pests and diseases, as the presence of multiple plant species creates a more complex environment that is less conducive to the spread of pathogens. This diversity also supports a wider range of beneficial insects, birds, and other wildlife, contributing to the overall health and balance of the garden. By creating a more biodiverse environment around peach trees, gardeners can reduce the likelihood of pest and disease outbreaks, leading to healthier trees and better fruit production.

Another benefit of companion planting is weed suppression. Low-growing companion plants, such as chives and nasturtiums, can act as living mulch, covering the soil and preventing weeds from taking hold. This reduces competition for nutrients, water, and sunlight, allowing the peach tree to thrive. In addition to suppressing weeds, these ground-covering plants help conserve soil moisture by reducing evaporation, which is particularly beneficial during hot, dry periods. This natural form of weed control reduces the need for manual weeding or herbicides, making garden maintenance easier and more environmentally friendly.

Companion planting contributes to a more aesthetically pleasing garden. The vibrant colors and varied textures of companion plants can create a visually appealing environment around peach trees, enhancing the overall beauty of the garden. The presence of flowers, herbs, and vegetables alongside peach trees adds interest and diversity to the landscape, making the garden a more enjoyable place to spend time. This aesthetic appeal, combined with the functional benefits of companion planting, makes it a valuable practice for any gardener looking to create a productive and beautiful garden space.

Designing a Peach Tree Guild

A peach tree guild is a thoughtfully designed planting system that combines peach trees with a variety of companion plants to create a self-sustaining, mutually beneficial ecosystem. The concept of a guild comes from permaculture, a design philosophy that emphasizes working with nature to create sustainable agricultural systems. In a peach tree guild, each plant in the system has a specific role, whether it's attracting pollinators, repelling pests, fixing nitrogen in the soil, or providing ground cover. The goal is to create a balanced, diverse environment where all the plants support each other, leading to healthier peach trees and a more productive garden.

The foundation of a peach tree guild is, of course, the peach tree itself, which serves as the central element around which the rest of the guild is built. When designing a guild, it's important to consider the specific needs of the peach tree, such as its sunlight, water, and nutrient requirements. The companion plants chosen for the guild should complement the peach tree

133

by providing additional resources or protection. For example, deep-rooted plants like comfrey can help bring up nutrients from the soil, while nitrogen-fixing plants like beans can enrich the soil with nitrogen.

Ground cover plants are an essential component of a peach tree guild. These low-growing plants help protect the soil from erosion, retain moisture, and suppress weeds. In a peach tree guild, suitable ground cover plants might include chives, nasturtiums, or creeping thyme. These plants not only cover the soil but also offer additional benefits, such as pest repellent properties or edible leaves and flowers. By choosing ground covers that fulfill multiple roles, gardeners can maximize the efficiency and productivity of the guild.

Herbs and flowers that attract beneficial insects play a vital role in a peach tree guild. Plants like marigolds, yarrow, and dill are excellent choices, as they attract pollinators and predatory insects that help control pest populations. These plants can be interspersed throughout the guild, providing bursts of color and fragrance while enhancing the overall health of the ecosystem. The presence of these insect-attracting plants ensures that the peach tree receives adequate pollination and protection from pests, leading to better fruit yields.

Nitrogen-fixing plants are another key element in a peach tree guild. These plants, such as clover, beans, or peas, have the ability to capture nitrogen from the air and convert it into a form that plants can use. Planting nitrogen-fixers near the peach tree helps improve soil fertility, reducing the need for synthetic fertilizers. These plants can be grown as cover crops or incorporated into the guild as permanent fixtures, depending on the gardener's preference and the specific needs of the peach tree.

Mulch plants, which provide organic matter for the soil, are also important in a peach tree guild. Comfrey is an excellent choice for this role, as it produces large amounts of biomass that can be cut back and used as mulch around the base of the peach tree. The decomposing leaves enrich the soil with nutrients, improve soil structure, and retain moisture. Other good mulch plants include alfalfa and borage, which also attract pollinators and beneficial insects.

When designing a peach tree guild, it's important to consider the layout and spacing of the plants to ensure that each one has enough room to grow and fulfill its role. Taller plants should be placed towards the back or center of the guild, where they won't shade out smaller plants. Ground covers and low-growing herbs can be planted around the base of the peach tree, while larger companion plants, like comfrey or yarrow, can be placed in the surrounding area. The design should allow for easy access to the peach tree for maintenance and harvesting.

Chapter 18

Additional Resources

Glossary of Terms Specific to Peach Trees Terminology

- **Budding**: A method of grafting where a single bud from one plant is inserted into the bark of another, allowing the bud to grow and develop into a new branch or tree.

- **Chill Hours**: The total number of hours below 45°F that a peach tree requires during its dormant period to produce fruit in the following growing season. Different varieties require different amounts of chill hours.

- **Clingstone**: A type of peach where the flesh clings tightly to the pit, making it more difficult to remove the stone from the flesh.

- **Dormant Spray**: A type of horticultural oil or fungicide applied during the dormant season to control overwintering pests and diseases on peach trees.

- **Freestone**: A type of peach where the flesh easily separates from the pit, making it easier to remove the stone from the flesh.

- **Grafting**: A method of propagation where a section of a stem with leaf buds is inserted into the stock of a tree, allowing the two to grow together.

- **Peach Leaf Curl**: A common fungal disease that causes the leaves of peach trees to become distorted, thickened, and discolored. Preventive fungicide sprays are typically applied in the dormant season to control this disease.

- **Pruning**: The practice of cutting away dead or overgrown branches or stems to encourage healthy growth and fruit production in peach trees.

- **Rootstock**: The root part of a grafted plant that provides the root system for a new plant, often chosen for its disease resistance, hardiness, or growth characteristics.

- **Scion**: A young shoot or twig of a peach tree that is grafted onto a rootstock to propagate a new tree with desirable characteristics.

- **Self-Fertile**: A peach tree variety that can pollinate itself without the need for another tree to produce fruit.

- **Suckers**: Unwanted shoots that grow from the base or roots of a peach tree, which can divert energy away from the main tree if not removed.

- **Thinning**: The process of removing excess fruit from a peach tree to ensure that the remaining fruit grows larger and reaches full maturity.

- **Vase Shape**: A common pruning technique for peach trees where the tree is shaped like a vase, with an open center to allow sunlight and air to reach the inner branches.

- **Stone Fruit**: A category of fruits, including peaches, that have a large, hard pit (stone) inside, surrounded by fleshy fruit.

Troubleshooting List & Quick Fixes for Common Problems

1. **Leaf Curl**:
   - ○ **Symptom**: Leaves become distorted, thickened, and take on a reddish hue.
   - ○ **Quick Fix**: Apply a copper-based fungicide during the dormant season to prevent infection. Once symptoms appear, remove affected leaves and avoid overwatering to reduce disease spread.

2. **Fruit Drop**:
   - ○ **Symptom**: Premature fruit falls from the tree before it fully ripens.
   - ○ **Quick Fix**: Ensure consistent watering, especially during dry periods. Thin excess fruit early in the season to reduce competition for nutrients. Check for nutrient deficiencies and apply a balanced fertilizer if needed.

3. **Aphid Infestation**:
   - ○ **Symptom**: Leaves become curled, sticky (due to honeydew), and covered in small, green or black insects.
   - ○ **Quick Fix**: Spray with insecticidal soap or neem oil. Encourage natural predators like ladybugs by planting companion plants such as marigolds or dill.

4. **Poor Fruit Set**:
   - ○ **Symptom**: Few fruits develop despite good flowering.
   - ○ **Quick Fix**: Ensure adequate pollination by attracting bees with flowering companion plants. Apply a balanced fertilizer to boost

tree health. Avoid excessive nitrogen, which can lead to lush foliage but poor fruit set.

5. **Brown Rot**:
   - o **Symptom**: Fruit develops brown spots that rapidly enlarge, and the fruit mummifies on the tree.
   - o **Quick Fix**: Prune to improve air circulation and remove any infected fruit. Apply a fungicide during bloom and pre-harvest. Avoid overhead watering to reduce moisture on the fruit.

6. **Sunscald**:
   - o **Symptom**: Bark on the sun-exposed side of the tree cracks, splits, or peels.
   - o **Quick Fix**: Paint the trunk with a 50/50 mixture of white latex paint and water to reflect sunlight. Mulch around the base of the tree to regulate soil temperature.

7. **Gummosis**:
   - o **Symptom**: Sap oozes from the bark, usually as a result of physical injury or disease.
   - o **Quick Fix**: Identify and remove the cause of the injury (e.g., insect damage or mechanical injury). Apply a fungicide if a fungal infection is suspected. Ensure proper watering to avoid stress.

8. **Wilting Leaves**:
   - o **Symptom**: Leaves wilt, curl, and may drop, especially during hot weather.

o **Quick Fix**: Water deeply and regularly, especially during heat waves. Check for root rot or poor drainage if wilting persists. Mulch to conserve moisture and reduce root temperature.

9. **Peach Scab**:

o **Symptom**: Small, dark spots appear on the fruit and twigs.

o **Quick Fix**: Prune to allow better air circulation and sunlight penetration. Apply a fungicide during early fruit development. Remove any affected fruit and leaves to reduce the spread.

10. **Frost Damage**:

o **Symptom**: Blossoms or young fruit are damaged or drop after a late frost.

o **Quick Fix**: Cover the tree with frost cloths or blankets during cold snaps. Water the tree thoroughly before a frost, as moist soil retains heat better than dry soil. Consider planting varieties with later bloom times in frost-prone areas.

Fun Fact List About Peach Trees

- **Ancient Origins**: Peaches have been cultivated for over 4,000 years, with their origins traced back to China, where they were considered a symbol of immortality and friendship.

- **World's Largest Peach**: The largest peach on record weighed over 1.75 pounds and was grown in California. Peaches typically weigh between 4 to 6 ounces, making this peach exceptionally large.

- **Georgia's Claim to Fame**: Georgia, USA, is nicknamed the "Peach State," but it's not the top peach-producing state. That title belongs to California, which produces over 50% of the peaches in the United States.

- **Variety Count**: There are over 2,000 varieties of peaches worldwide, with differences in size, color, flavor, and whether they are freestone or clingstone.

- **Peach Flowering**: Peaches are among the first fruit trees to bloom in the spring, often showcasing beautiful pink blossoms that attract pollinators and add early color to gardens.

- **Peach Pit Myth**: It's a common myth that peach pits are deadly if ingested. While the pits do contain cyanogenic compounds, one would have to eat many crushed pits to ingest a harmful dose.

- **Cultural Significance**: In Chinese culture, peaches are associated with longevity and vitality. They are often depicted in art and folklore as a symbol of immortality.

- **Cloning Through Grafting**: Most commercial peach trees are not grown from seed but are grafted. This technique ensures that the fruit produced is consistent in quality and taste from year to year.

- **Nutrient-Rich**: Peaches are not only delicious but also packed with nutrients like vitamins A and C, potassium, and dietary fiber, making them a healthy addition to any diet.

- **Record-Breaking Harvest**: The largest peach orchard in the world is located in South Carolina, USA, and spans over 1,300 acres, producing millions of pounds of peaches annually.

FAQ Related to Peach Tree Treatment

Q: How often should I water my peach tree?

A: Water your peach tree deeply once a week, providing enough water to moisten the soil to a depth of 2 to 3 feet. During hot, dry periods, you may need to water more frequently. Young trees require more frequent watering, about twice a week, until they are well-established.

Q: What is the best fertilizer for peach trees?

A: A balanced fertilizer with equal parts nitrogen, phosphorus, and potassium (such as 10-10-10) is ideal for peach trees. Apply it in early spring as the tree begins to grow and again in late spring or early summer. Be careful not to over-fertilize, as too much nitrogen can lead to excessive vegetative growth at the expense of fruit production.

Q: How do I prevent peach leaf curl?

A: To prevent peach leaf curl, apply a copper-based fungicide during the tree's dormant period, typically in late fall or early winter. Make sure to thoroughly cover the branches, trunk, and buds to protect against this fungal disease.

Q: When is the best time to prune peach trees?

A: The best time to prune peach trees is in late winter or early spring, just before the tree breaks dormancy and begins to bud. Pruning during this time minimizes the risk of disease and encourages vigorous new growth.

Q: Can I grow a peach tree from a pit?

A: Yes, you can grow a peach tree from a pit, but the resulting tree may not produce fruit identical to the parent. To grow from a pit, remove and clean the seed, stratify it in the refrigerator for several weeks, and then plant it in a pot or directly in the ground.

Q: How do I know when my peaches are ready to harvest?

A: Peaches are ready to harvest when they develop a deep color (depending on the variety), have a slight give when gently squeezed, and emit a sweet fragrance. The fruit should easily separate from the branch when twisted gently.

Q: Why are my peaches small and underdeveloped?

A: Small, underdeveloped peaches can result from overcrowding on the tree, lack of water, or nutrient deficiencies. Thinning the fruit early in the season, ensuring consistent watering, and applying a balanced fertilizer can help improve fruit size and quality.

Q: What can I do about peach tree borers?

A: To control peach tree borers, apply a preventive insecticide to the lower trunk and base of the tree in late spring or early summer, when the adult borers are laying eggs. Keeping the tree healthy through proper watering, fertilization, and pruning also helps it resist borer damage.

Q: My peach tree's leaves are turning yellow. What could be the problem?

A: Yellowing leaves on a peach tree can indicate overwatering, nutrient deficiencies (particularly nitrogen or iron), or poor drainage. Check the soil moisture levels and adjust watering as needed. Consider testing the soil and applying the appropriate fertilizer to address any nutrient deficiencies.

Q: Do I need more than one peach tree for fruit production?

A: Most peach tree varieties are self-fertile, meaning they do not require another tree for pollination to produce fruit. However, planting multiple varieties can increase fruit yield and extend the harvest season.

Daily, Weekly, Monthly, and Seasonal Care Tasks Summary

Daily Care:

- Monitor soil moisture levels and adjust watering as needed, especially during hot weather.
- Check for signs of pests or diseases, such as curled leaves, discoloration, or the presence of insects.
- Remove any fallen leaves, fruit, or debris from around the tree to reduce the risk of disease.

Weekly Care:

- Water the tree deeply once a week, ensuring the soil is moist to a depth of 2 to 3 feet.
- Inspect the tree for any new growth that may need training or pruning, particularly suckers or water sprouts.
- Mulch around the base of the tree to retain moisture and suppress weeds.

Monthly Care:

- Apply a balanced fertilizer according to the tree's growth stage and the season (spring and summer are critical times).
- Prune any dead or damaged branches to maintain the tree's shape and health.

- Conduct a thorough pest and disease check, treating any issues promptly with appropriate organic or chemical controls.

Seasonal Care

- **Spring**:
  - Fertilize the tree as it breaks dormancy to encourage new growth.
  - Prune to shape the tree and remove any dead or diseased wood.
  - Begin thinning the fruit once it is about the size of a nickel to ensure larger, healthier peaches.
- **Summer**:
  - Water regularly and deeply, especially during dry periods.
  - Continue thinning fruit if necessary to prevent overcrowding.
  - Monitor for signs of pests and diseases, applying treatments as needed.
  - Harvest peaches when they reach peak ripeness.
- **Autumn**:
  - Clean up fallen leaves and fruit to reduce the risk of overwintering pests and diseases.
  - Apply a low-nitrogen fertilizer to strengthen the tree's roots before winter.
  - Begin preparing the tree for winter by reducing watering and applying a fresh layer of mulch.

- **Winter**:
  - Prune the tree during dormancy to maintain its shape and promote healthy growth in the spring.
  - Apply dormant oil sprays to control overwintering pests.
  - Protect the tree from frost damage by wrapping the trunk and adding extra mulch around the base.
  - Continue monitoring for any signs of disease or damage and address them promptly.

Printed in Great Britain
by Amazon

62490228R00087